DI

This book is designed to provide information on stillbirth only. This information is provided and sold with the knowledge that the publisher and author do not offer any legal or medical advice. In the case of a need for any such expertise, consult with the appropriate professional. This book does not contain all information available on the subject. This book has not been created to be specific to any individual's or organization's situation or needs. Every effort has been made to make this book as accurate as possible. However, there may be typographical and/or content errors. Therefore, this book should serve only as a general guide and not as the ultimate source of subject information. This book contains information that might be dated and is intended only to educate and entertain. The author and publisher shall have no liability or responsibility to any person or entity regarding any loss or damage incurred, or alleged to have incurred, directly or indirectly, by the information contained in this book. You hereby agree to be bound by this disclaimer or you may return this book within the guarantee time period for a full refund. In the interest of full disclosure, this book may contain affiliate links that might pay the author or publisher a commission upon any purchase from the company. While the author and publisher take no responsibility for the business practices of these companies and or the performance of any product or service, the author or publisher has used the product or service and makes a recommendation in good faith based on that experience. All characters appearing in this work have given permission or are fictitious. Any resemblance to real persons, living or dead, is purely coincidental. The opinions and stories in this book are the views of the author and not that of the publisher.

DEDICATION

For Kegan, who I hold in my heart,
Keira, who I hold in my arms,
and Karol, who holds my hand.

ACKNOWLEDGMENTS

Writing a book was far more challenging and also far more rewarding than I ever could have imagined. I could not have written this book solely on my own, and its publishing is due to the collective effort of a large body of people. I would like to thank the many individuals who supported, challenged, and pushed me while I immersed myself in writing.

First off, I must begin by thanking my wonderful husband, Karol. Thank you for reading every chapter as soon as I finished it, thank you for constantly being willing to relive the death of your son so I could write a book, thank you for never wavering in your belief of me. Thank you for supporting me when I buried myself in both updating medical guidelines and passing a law, and thank you especially for your immense faith in me when I did not always have it in myself. And always, always, thank you for making me laugh and thank you for all the kitchen dances. You are my person.

To my beautiful daughter, Keira, thank you for filling every day with more joy than I knew existed in this world. Thank you for your immense patience with Mama as I advocate against stillbirth; thank you for attending meetings with congressmen and women, thank you for understanding when I have a stillbirth meeting, and thank you for continuing to keep your brother present in your heart and mind. I will never be able to apologize enough that I wasn't able to give you your brother to grow with; you deserve the world and I wish I had been able to give you Kegan. I am so proud of who you are becoming.

To Lisa Proehl, my grief mentor, the inspiration for the character of Sarah, and my dear friend, thank you for your guidance, love, and literary feedback. I don't know who I would be or how I would have survived this strange grief landscape without you. You brought light and order into the darkest, most chaotic times. Thank you for how much you delight in both of my children. Your sweet Sophie has made such an impact on my life.

To Blair Carter, thank you for your reading the entire manuscript in one night (!) and for your support and helpful comments. Thank you for reaching out when I lost Kegan, and thank you for guiding me in those first months. I think of Hazel all the time.

I am incredibly grateful to numerous organizations and individuals for their work in stillbirth prevention and grief advocacy. The work of the BeliEve Foundation, Star Legacy Foundation, Now I Lay Me Down to Sleep, and the International Stillbirth Alliance informed so many aspects of this book. These organizations are examples of what it means to truly make a difference in the world and to lift people during their darkest hours.

Lastly, to my editing and publishing team: Richter Publishing, where would I be without you! Thank you for bringing this story to the world! I am so grateful to have had the opportunity to work with you and for your immensely helpful comments and suggestions.

To the many friends and family members who I didn't list but who still hold a special place in my heart: thank you for your support, love, patience, tears, and laughter. Stillbirth is a special kind of grief, it's a grief that seems invisible to the outside observer, but one that tears the griever to shreds. Thank you for being willing to listen and learn. Thank you for loving my son, thank you for loving my daughter, and thank you for supporting our family.

Table of Contents

DISCLAIMER 3

DEDICATION 4

ACKNOWLEDGMENTS 5

INTRODUCTION 10

PROLOGUE: LOSING KEGAN 12

CHAPTER 1: ON GRIEF 20

CHAPTER 2: ON MENTAL AND PHYSICAL HEALTH 37

CHAPTER 3: ON LOGISTICS AND PRACTICAL CONSIDERATIONS 55

CHAPTER 4: ON THE PREVENTABILITY OF STILLBIRTH 73

CHAPTER 5: ON SOCIAL SUPPORT AFTER STILLBIRTH 90

CHAPTER 6: ON ROMANTIC RELATIONSHIPS AFTER STILLBIRTH 111

CHAPTER 7: ON SIBLINGS OF THE STILLBORN INFANT 129

CHAPTER 8: ON GRIEF TRIGGERS 149

CHAPTER 9: ON HOLIDAYS AND ANNIVERSARIES 166

CHAPTER 10: ON GRIEF OVER TIME 183

KEGAN'S KINDNESS 198

STILLBIRTH AND GRIEF RESOURCES 200

REFERENCES 202

ABOUT THE AUTHOR 210

INTRODUCTION

Still His Mama was inspired by our family's lived experience with stillbirth. In the fall of 2018, I was nine months pregnant when our son's heart suddenly stopped beating in utero. Our son, Kegan Christopher Hatzilias, was stillborn mere days before his due date.

After Kegan's death, my husband and I scoured the available medical literature for resources both to guide us through the grief process, and to help us understand stillbirth. We desperately wanted to feel connected to other grieving parents, to know we weren't alone in the loss of our child. Moreover, we wanted to know how we became the 1 in 160 [1] U.S. births that ends in a stillbirth, and what could be done to prevent future stillbirths. We were searching for guidance, answers, and empathy.

It is through connecting with a grief therapist and other bereaved parents that we have slowly begun to piece our days back together. Every day we attempt to learn the shape of our new life; a life we never wanted, but that is ours nonetheless. Some days we learn with the help of others and some days we have to learn alone, but every day we are learning what a life without our son looks like.

In the early days of grief, I found that sometimes I simply didn't have the strength to hold conversations with other bereaved parents. I would desperately want to connect but found the mental and emotional energy of a conversation was more than my shattered heart, mind, and body could handle. That place, the place of wanting a conversation surrounding stillbirth and grief, but being unable to engage in one, is where this book comes from.

Still His Mama is part memoir, part medical literature review, and part journaling assistant. This work draws both on my personal experience as a bereaved mother and my professional experience as a neuroscientist and medical writer to explore the world of stillbirth and its subsequent heartbreak. Still His Mama addresses ten themes related to stillbirth and grief, with each chapter focusing on a specific aspect of the stillbirth experience.

Still His Mama is organized in a format that allows both personal and scientific explorations of each theme discussed. The first half of each chapter is dedicated to fictional letters as imagined between two bereaved mothers, one of whom is newly bereaved and the other who lost her child to stillbirth nearly twenty years prior. The letter format allows for the rawness, intensity, and complexity of parental grief to be openly shared in a way the reader can easily relate to. The second half of each chapter is devoted to my own personal experience with the topic, as well as a discussion of pertinent medical literature. In this section, I offer my own insight on each theme, as well as an analysis of what the science (as of 2021) tells us about it. Finally, each chapter concludes with a journaling prompt to inspire introspective reflection on the theme explored. In this manner, my hope is that a grief-stricken parent can relate to and mentally engage in a conversation on stillbirth and their baby on the days when they simply do not have the capability to have an actual conversation.

If you are reading this book with a lost child in mind, I am so sorry it is relevant to you. I wish from the bottom of my heart that you had your baby in your arms instead of a book. As that is not the path our lives have taken, my wish instead is that you will never feel alone in your grief and that you will know your child is never forgotten.

In heartbreak,

Terrell (Kegan's mama, forever)

---

[1] Per 2020 data from American College of Obstetricians and Gynecologists and The Society for Maternal-Fetal Medicine

PROLOGUE: LOSING KEGAN

His life started as a typical pregnancy. The first trimester was difficult, but not impossible. I was tired and nauseated, unable to nap while simultaneously running around after our two-year-old daughter. The nausea disappeared by week nine, and during his eleventh week I felt his first magical flutters in my belly. He was strong for his age, kicking early and often, a sign we took for him being an extremely healthy baby. At the 20-week anatomy scan, we had our first moment of worry when we learned he was a single umbilical artery, or two-vessel, baby. The umbilical cord, which usually has one vein and two arteries, had only one artery. Our doctors, however, assured us this was no cause for concern. We had performed genetic testing on him early on and knew he had no chromosomal anomalies, and that there were no other morphological warning signs. Our doctors classified him as an "isolated single umbilical artery baby" and promised us there was no reason to panic as long as he was growing well. And grow well he did! Our son measured at or around the 50th percentile persistently, exactly as his big sister had measured during her pregnancy. As an additional precaution, I started going to the doctor multiple times a week beginning at week 34 for twice weekly non-stress tests and weekly ultrasounds. According to medical guidelines, this degree of monitoring wasn't necessary for two-vessel babies (if anything, our frequent visits were seen as paranoid by some), but we had chosen a cautious doctor and she shared our desire to keep a close eye on our little one. We didn't want to risk anything going wrong with our precious little boy, our sweet Polliwog, and besides, with the extra monitoring I got to hear his musical heartbeat thrice weekly. I had no idea then how much I would treasure the memory of his perfect, steady heartbeat.

The day we lost him was a standard day. I was just over 38 weeks along and going in for another non-stress test. His big sister and I had a relaxing walk through the park early that morning and when her babysitter arrived, I cheerfully drove off to the doctor, excited to hear the steady bumbum of my son's little heart. When the nurse strapped the monitoring belt onto me, she had a difficult time finding his heart...was he head down? Had he flipped? Yes, he had been head down for weeks, ready to be born. My own heart rate shot up as she rapidly moved the belt across my swollen belly, searching for the music from his little heart. When the radiology tech with the portable Doppler entered the room, I felt my eyes fill with tears, felt my throat tighten with panic. I had already withdrawn into my own world by the time she uttered the four worst words in the English language, "There is no heartbeat." I heard an anguished cry of "NO! No no no!" and felt the floor fall away. How could this be? I was so careful during pregnancy, so paranoid even, this wasn't happening. In a fog, I watched my doctor enter the room, sadness and confusion written across her face. I demanded they try again, they had to be wrong, he was ALIVE that morning, he had kicked his daddy just that morning. He was healthy and strong, he was due any day, they just had to be wrong. I'll never forget the look of sadness she gave me as she agreed to look for his heartbeat again. I didn't need her to say anything the second time—I could read the machine. There was no heartbeat.

When you lose a baby at term, you still have to deliver him. You still have to go through labor. I asked my doctor what happened to us next and she explained I was going to be induced. Did I want to wait until tomorrow? No, better just to get it over with. Better to hold him in my arms soon, instead of feeling his stillness in my stomach all evening. I texted my husband to call me and he hurriedly responded, no doubt expecting to hear me tell him I was in labor and he needed to come to the hospital because our son was going to be born soon. He was right, all those things were true...except our son was already dead.

Together we walked over to Labor and Delivery. Walked past the sound of other women laboring to deliver their healthy, living children. Walked past the sound of newborns crying and excited parents welcoming their child with love and exhaustion in their voices. Walked past the future that was supposed to be ours. Our room was nice enough, typical for delivery. A bed. A bathroom. A sink. A couch for him. Nothing unusual except the somber faces of the nurses as they shuffled in and out, and the rainbow hung on the door to indicate loss. Enter carefully, it said. Heartbreak lives here.

I asked for an epidural for delivery—I figured there was no point in experiencing more pain at that point and part of me hoped it would help numb the gash across my heart. A foolish hope, a hope born of extreme pain, extreme confusion, and extreme loss. The epidural only partially worked, a blessing and a curse in one. At least this way I got to experience some of him—if labor and delivery was all of him I'd get, I was glad to feel some of it. If labor and delivery was all of mothering him I was allowed, I was glad to have memory of it. As labor progressed, I became convinced the doctors were wrong. Surely, he would be born breathing. Surely, he would be born with as strong a heartbeat as he had always had, wailing his displeasure at his abrupt coldness, surprising everyone in the room except his mama, who would laughingly welcome his squirming body into her arms. I was wrong. As he ripped his way out of my body, the only sound in the room was the nurse asking my husband if he wanted to cut the cord. He quietly shook his head.

His tiny body was perfect. He was six pounds, ten ounces and twenty inches of perfection. A baby. Not a lost pregnancy, not a sad event that happened to us, but a perfect, beautiful, take your breath away baby. A human being. He had my nose and ears, and his daddy's thick, dark, wavy hair. His cheeks were chubby and pinchable, just as a newborn's should be. His rosebud lips were slightly redder than expected, the only indication of death. I bent my head and kissed those perfect lips. My baby. My son. Our son. Kegan Christopher, born at 12:53 am on November 7, 2018.

The next few hours are permanently seared into my brain. My husband sobbing with pain as he gazed at his son, myself alternating between begging him to open his eyes and gently stroking his petal soft newborn skin. My fingers softly booping his tiny nose, and my husband's lips gently kissing his perfect fingers. The two of us sang our family lullabies to him, the ones we would sing to his sister every naptime and every evening, the ones he had heard daily for the past nine months. After four hours, the effects of death started to show upon his skin. As they wrapped him up to take him away to the morgue, the sobs tore themselves out of my throat, "My baby, my baby! Oh my baby!"

There is a wonderful organization called Now I Lay Me Down to Sleep that provides professional quality photographs of recently deceased newborns. When our photographer was able to make it the next morning, Kegan was brought back to us from the morgue. I'll never forget how cold his skin felt, more evidence that his goodbye was final, that his death was permanent and real. The photographer quietly took photos of the three of us, and then solemnly packed up his equipment and left. My husband and I returned to stroking Kegan's sweet face, marveling at his adorable fingers and toes, and kissing that perfect, miniature nose. After a few hours, we realized it was time to say our last farewell to our boy. We called the nurse in and she began wrapping him up. "Make sure he's warm enough," I begged, "we don't want him to be cold, he's just a baby." She placed him in a bassinet and wheeled him out of the room to the sounds of our broken voices serenading him with our family lullaby. As soon as the door closed, we broke down in sobs. When I learned Kegan was dead, I thought the hardest thing I would ever have to do was deliver my dead child. Again, I was wrong—harder than that was giving him back. Harder than his birth was his final goodbye.

We left the hospital as soon as we could that afternoon. There was no point in staying once we had said goodbye to Kegan, and we needed to get away from the building that only symbolized death and loss to us. The next few days were a blur. Postpartum pain, the typical heavy bleeding after delivery coupled with a razor continually slicing my heart open. My breasts cruelly filling with milk and me crying out to my husband, "My body doesn't know he's dead!" My returning thinness a visible reminder of my body's failure to keep our child alive. At times shock took over, saving us from completely losing our minds to the overwhelming grief in our hearts. In those moments, it felt like we were watching an incredibly sad movie about a family experiencing an unimaginable loss. The shock would always wear off, crashing us into the canyon of our grief again. My husband took over most of the childcare of our daughter in those early days, immersing himself in her laughter and games. After she went to sleep at night, we would hold onto each other and cry, trying to keep our tears quiet enough not to disturb her innocent rest.

The early days of support we received from the majority of our family and friends was genuine and gracious, life-affirming and full of love. My cousin and his family kept our two-year-old happy, safe, and distracted while we were in the hospital. Local friends and acquaintances we had known for barely a year set up a meal delivery train, frozen foods and restaurant gift cards arrived from multiple sets of friends across the country, toys and books were sent to our toddler, and mementos depicting Kegan's sweet, precious features immediately showed up at our doorstep. We treasured and continue to treasure the support we have received. People who didn't just say "let me know if I can help," but who instead took it upon themselves to ensure that we ate and had physical keepsakes of our son will forever hold a special place in our hearts. Some people did offer empty platitudes, "we're here for you" they would say, but would offer nothing to help us maintain our grip on reality, nothing to acknowledge they understood the gravity of our loss. In fairness, how could they? How could anyone except another bereaved parent begin to understand the pain of losing your child? And then, of course, there were those who looked away and simply wished for our silence, those who didn't understand our intensity of grief over losing someone who was only here for such a short while, someone we didn't have years of memories with to mourn. But then, we also didn't have years of memories in which to take solace. The thing about losing your baby is, you don't just lose them at their babyhood. You lose them at every step in their life, you lose every memory you had already dreamed of making with them. We had pencil sketch dreams of a life with our son, and we had waited eagerly for him to animate them with his own rich colors and details. Now we had to erase the page.

The autopsy results confirmed what we already knew: Kegan was perfect. The cause of his death was ruled to be an umbilical cord accident. His death was rapid and painless; a blood clot formed at a twist in his cord, he sleepily settled in for a nap, and within minutes, our sweet boy was gone. Even if we had witnessed the moment of clotting, the moment his oxygen was cut off, an emergency c-section wouldn't have been fast enough to have saved him. His death was a freak accident, a statistical anomaly. Statistically speaking, he shouldn't have died. But then, what do statistics matter to the individual? I am grateful, however, that the cause of his death was identified. For the first six weeks after his death, we had no idea what caused it. Those six weeks were pure hell as I obsessively recounted every second leading up to his little heart's stillness, torturing my husband and myself with potential causes of death. The knowledge that I was not to blame for his death alleviated the guilt to some extent but did nothing to quell the devastation in our hearts. Despite knowing that I didn't cause his death and couldn't have saved him, I still obsess over the question of why…why did this happen to us? I was so cautious…why couldn't I keep him safe? On the off-chance that I'm not berating myself over his death, someone will invariably raise the issue on their own. "What happened?" they say. What did you do wrong, they mean. How did you lose a healthy baby at term? I've learned to rapidly change the subject. Curiosity is not the burden of the bereaved.

As time has gone on, I worry that we have used up our allotted grief time, that our overwhelming sadness makes people wish we would hurry up and get over it already. Sympathetic silences have turned to judgment in the guise of concern, a palpable irritation at the permanent changes wrought inside of us and our inability to return to our pre-Kegan selves. A sense of confusion, sometimes even anger, at our refusal to return to previous priorities, at our insistence in honoring our son, slowly seeps its way into conversations. We observe these changes and wistfully move on from fractured relationships with a sharp sense of betrayal at the further, unnecessary losses. We are not who we were before November 6, 2018; the old versions of us died with our son. As there is no getting over his death, there is no going back to who we used to be. We are permanently altered, seared by the death of a child no one else met, a child no one else really knew…a child no one else fully mourns. Our agony is singular, confined to our battered hearts alone.

We have a daily struggle of reconciling ourselves to the fact that we have two children, but only one of them is living. This is our reality and will remain so for the rest of our lives. How do you begin a day when the first thing you think of every morning is the death of your son? How can you live a life when every day begins with your heart shattering anew? You are always acutely aware of everything he SHOULD be doing. About now he would be smiling for the first time. About now he would be learning how to crawl. Maybe he would finally be sleeping through the night now. You have an inexpressible rage at mothers who are careless with their pregnancies, at fathers who flippantly complain about the petty grievances of parenthood, at all parents who so easily take it for granted that their child lived, while you, cautious to a fault you, are inexplicably left with empty arms.

After the death of your child, a primal need to continue parenting them in any manner remaining to you develops. There are so few ways left to the bereaved to parent their child, so few ways to feel an active connection with your baby, to try to fill the ever-growing chasm in your heart. We participate in walks in Kegan's honor, we create memory boxes and mementos for him, we help our daughter blow bubbles to him on family holidays...we are constantly scanning the horizon for any way to include him. Family photos, previously a joyful experience, become filled with anxiety and heartbreak, a visible reminder that one member of the family will always be missing. That one member of the family will never grow. The days leading up to the anniversaries of his death and birth become drenched in sadness and apprehension, a stark contrast to the overwhelming joy and anticipation those same days held just a short time ago. And then his birthday...how do you celebrate the birth of a child who was born dead? How do you celebrate the life of a baby who never got to open his eyes? How do you give him the legacy he deserves? We have chosen to dedicate his birthday to performing acts of charity and kindness and have asked others to join in. My husband dubbed this movement "Kegan's Kindness," a gentle, active tribute to the good we know our son would have brought into the world. We do these things in desperate attempts to both connect with our baby and to remind the world that our child existed, that our son mattered. Mostly, we do these things in our anguished struggle to parent the child whose shoes we will never tie, whose tears we will never dry, and whose giggle we will never know. These acts aren't enough, nothing could ever be enough, but they are all we will ever have.

In my mind, there exists a multitude of visions of our dark-haired little boy, growing up in the world that should have been his. In one of them he is eight months old, with chubby thighs the size of Michelin tires. He sits up giggling, knocking stacking rings over. His round eyes are squinted in laughter as the rings scatter across the room. He is perfect. In another, he is nine years old, skating off the ice after a victorious hockey game. His sweaty dark curls bounce around his eyes as they laughingly meet mine. He is healthy, full of life, and tremendously loved. One of those things will remain forever true.

CHAPTER 1: ON GRIEF

"Grief, I've learned, is really just love. It's all the love you want to give, but cannot. All that unspent love gathers up in the corners of your eyes, the lump in your throat, and in that hollow part of your chest. Grief is just love with no place to go."

~Jamie Anderson

My dear Evelyn,

Sweet mama, I was so sorry to hear of the loss of your son, your precious baby boy Liam. My own daughter, Madeline, was born sleeping seventeen years ago and I can still feel the weight of her body in my arms and see the curve of her perfect forehead when I close my eyes. I was given your name by your neighbor and my sister, Rose, and hope it is alright for me to reach out to you.

When I lost Maddie, I felt simultaneously as if a spotlight had been shown on me in my darkest hour, and as if I had been locked in a room to grieve alone, as if the intensity of my grief was unwelcome in a world that looks away when babies die. I want you to know, you don't have to grieve alone. We who have lost our children in this way can hold each other up until we each learn to stand again. I would love to hear more about Liam, and your tender mama heart. I hope to hear from you, and please know that I am holding you, Liam, and your entire family in my heart and mind.

A fellow grieving mama,

Sarah

Sarah,

Thank you for your kind letter. I don't know where to begin, never having expected or prepared myself for this reality. It doesn't even feel like a reality yet, it still feels like a dream—or rather, a nightmare. Every day I wake up and expect Liam to be in his bassinet, every day I wake up and have to remind myself he is dead...and so every day, he dies for me again.

I so wish I could take his place, that it could be me who had been wheeled into the morgue instead of him, that my heart had been the one that stopped instead of his, but...I can't. I can't. The unfairness of it all is overwhelming. His heart stopped and mine shattered, and somehow, inexplicably, mine kept beating, but oh! How I wish it hadn't.

Simultaneously, I feel incredibly guilty for these feelings as I know my husband, David, and Liam's big sister, Lyra, need me, especially now. I can't process this for them or myself—I'm in complete shock. Some days I wake up and can't remember the day prior, and some days I wake up thinking I am still pregnant before the truth comes crashing down again. Our home, always so happy and light, is full of heartbreak and heaviness. I can't imagine how we will begin to heal, and moreover I don't know if I want to.

In heartbreak,

Evelyn

My dear Evelyn,

Oh sweet mama, I wish I could reach through these pages and hug you. I hear you so strongly. The paradoxical nature of grief is that it isolates us while simultaneously making us feel conspicuous. After Maddie's death, I felt as if every aspect of our day-to-day lives were highlighted and scrutinized, yet I also felt profoundly alone. Every movement, every expression or gesture seemed to be a statement to the world on my mental state, and none of them seemed right or correct. I remember feeling self-conscious and guilty if I smiled ("how can she smile? Her baby is dead," the world seemed to shout), and also feeling self-conscious and guilty when I was sad ("try to focus on the positive, be grateful for what you have," the world would lecture). I constantly struggled with learning HOW to grieve, with trying to find the "right" way to grieve in a society that is so unwelcoming and intolerant of grief. Every perceived misstep, every gentle "correction" offered by an uncomfortable or even well-meaning friend seemed to be evidence of further alienation from a society I no longer fit into, from a world from which I had fractured.

It was only through time that I learned the truth—there is no right way to grieve. There is only survival.

Grief is not a journey with an end destination. It is a lifelong condition; a constant state of yearning for the one you have lost. I kept waiting to stop missing Maddie until I finally realized the truth—I'm not meant to stop missing her. I am her mother and I will love and miss her every day for the rest of my life. Just as you are Liam's mother and you will love and miss him every day for the rest of your life, and that, sweet mama, is the beauty of a mother's love. It lasts forever. Grief doesn't end because love never ends.

There is a misperception that grief is restricted to the intense period of mourning that follows the immediate aftermath of death and that after a (very short!) defined period of time, the griever's life returns to a static, normal, pre-death condition. While well-meaning, this perception puts an undue burden on the griever to hurry through the "work" of mourning and to get back to their previous life. I'm here to tell you, you don't have to rush through anything. Feel whatever you feel, whenever you feel it, and share it with whomever you desire. You are going through fire—you don't have to worry about protecting the rest of the world from a little heat.

Yours in loss,

Sarah

Dear Sarah,

How do you explain the pain that comes from stillbirth to those who have never experienced it? I constantly struggle with having to convey the uniqueness of heartbreak from giving birth to a stillborn baby. So many losses involve losing the life you knew, but when you lose a child, especially when you lose a baby, you lose both the life you knew and the life you planned. A life no one else knew at all.

From an outside viewpoint, our day-to-day hasn't changed. We still drop Lyra off at preschool, work, pick her up at the end of the day, play with her in the evening, and then we all eat as a family and go to bed. Nothing LOOKS different. It doesn't look as if anyone is missing, but in actuality there is a monstrous hole tearing its way through every fiber of our beings. From the outside, it doesn't look as if there has been a great alteration in our lives. And yet...our lives are profoundly altered in every way imaginable. It is like screaming at the top of your lungs and then finding out your audience is deaf. No one can see the hole in our lives, because to them, our lives look identical to what they were before Liam's death. Of course, this is a false mirage, an image we paint to keep ourselves from falling apart and to keep Lyra's days as light as we are able. The truth is that we are constantly falling into the chasm Liam's death tore through our hearts.

Our day-to-day life may not look like a huge alteration from the life we were living before losing Liam, but we spend every moment drowning in *a deep and profound yearning for a perfect little boy with a head full of dark curls and a button nose. We spend every day thinking what our lives SHOULD be. Here we should be exhausted from night feedings, here we should be reminding Lyra to use gentle hands with the baby, here he should be finding his smile for the first time...here he should be, here he should be, here he will NEVER be, and no one feels his absence but us.*

Our lives have screeched to a halt since his death. We were already mentally living the life where we were able to bring him home from the hospital. That life never had a chance to materialize and to grieve it alone is so isolating. It feels as if the rest of the world cannot see the depth of our grief. It is as if to them, I just stopped being pregnant, whereas we know the truth. Our son died.

How on Earth do you begin to explain the depth of pain that accompanies a child's death to a world that never met your child?

In confusion,

Evelyn

Evelyn,

How do you explain the pain that comes with losing a stillborn child to the world...I wish I knew. In my seventeen years since Maddie's death, all I can say is, you cannot. Not completely. You can give windows of insight, little glimpses into our world, but unless someone has lived this experience, they will never truly understand what it means to live a life without their child.

Don't underestimate those windows of insight, however. While it is true that others may never fully understand what it means to lose a child, those windows can grow their awareness. For those who are willing to see, the insights you offer can grow both their empathy and general understanding of grief. Hopefully they will never experience this specific grief, but one day, they will grieve the loss of someone they love. We will all eventually bury someone we love; we will all grieve. I see part of Maddie's legacy as being an ambassador of grief. My husband, Paul, and I do not shy from sharing our grief with the world. We share it willingly and with love, hoping to reduce the burden our society has placed upon the grieving by reducing the stigma associated with grief. Your grief is proof of your love.

You are right, it is impossible to explain the unique, soul-wrenching pain associated with losing a child to stillbirth. It is impossible to convey the magnitude and complexities of this unique grief. But that does not mean you need to hide or silence it. If you have the desire to share, then feel free to share your heart, and know that someone is learning what grief looks like from you and that it does not have to be silenced. Know that somewhere down the road, you have lifted another hurting soul by the simple act of sharing your love.

You speak of feeling alone in your grief, that it appears as if the day-to-day of your life hasn't changed since Liam's death, and that all your turmoil is internal. Sweet mama, society may tell you your world hasn't changed, but I am here to tell you what you, David, and Lyra already know. Your world has changed. It has. You were pregnant for nine months, and then gave birth to a beautiful baby boy. You lost your son. Your world has changed.

You and David lost your baby son and Lyra lost her baby brother. These things are true whether or not society is prepared to address the magnitude of them. And further, you suffered a multitude of additional losses. Your letter describes isolation, loneliness, yearning, and confusion. These emotions speak to the innumerable, invisible losses that accompany grief. I so wish the pain of grief and the many losses it ushers in were spoken of more clearly in society. While we, the mourners, are preoccupied just trying to survive, grief reaches its insidious fingers into every facet of our lives, completely reshaping the world in its image.

After Maddie's death, I was shocked by the pure volume of losses I endured. The most obvious and striking of course was the loss of Maddie herself, the loss of my gorgeous baby girl and the life we had planned to share with her. And then there were all the collateral losses, losses I didn't even realize I had accumulated until years had passed.

I lost my identity. Was I still a mother? If I didn't have my baby girl to raise, was I a mama? The answer to this was (and is!) yes, but oh how hard to answer that question those first years! Was I a mother if I didn't have my baby? What did it mean to be her mother, and how could I parent her in her absence? How do you begin to parent without your child?

I lost my sense of family structure. How could I define the structure of our family in Maddie's absence? We were supposed to be Any Family. Any Family, on Any Street, in Any Town. Any happy, busy, stressed, silly, whole Family. And, before Maddie's death, we WERE Any Family. And then, all of a sudden, we weren't. In a second, we went from Any Family to the family that is mentioned in hushed tones behind turned heads... "did you hear about their baby?" they would say, "such a tragedy." Our family structure never had plans to include an urn or tombstone. Our holiday pictures never had plans to include a photo between us instead of a little girl. What does it mean when your family structure includes a dead child? How do you picture the shape of your family? How do you come to love the shape of your family when it includes a giant hole? But, once upon a time, we were Any Family. And then, suddenly, we weren't.

I lost my support system. We can discuss this more as it does or doesn't arise for you, but I will say it is a rare parent who doesn't lose a (or multiple!) friends or family members following the death of their child. After Maddie's death, Paul and my grief counselor warned us "your address book will change." We didn't believe this at first, but our counselor was absolutely correct. Change our address book did! I only mention this so that if and when this happens for you, you will not blame yourself. Grief strains relationships. It is not your fault. All you need to do is survive. Find the people who help you keep your head above water and focus on them.

I lost my sense of safety in the world. Prior to Maddie's death, I believed that if I behaved a certain way, I and the people I loved would be safe. If I did not take unnecessary risks, if I always played it safe, I would be safe, and moreover, so would the people who I loved. After Maddie died, I learned that wasn't true. Sometimes, you can be the safest, most careful person in existence, and it will not matter. Sometimes you can do everything right, beyond right, and the odds will still turn against you. This was a huge shock to me and completely altered my view of the world. I had always believed that if I did everything I was supposed to, if I was safe and careful, the world would respond accordingly. It almost destroyed me to realize that is not the case. And yet. And yet...the realization that I, I who was obsessively (and to the people around me, certainly irritatingly), careful with my pregnancy, could still lose a full-term child opened my eyes in a way I had never imagined. If the world was this unpredictable for me, perhaps it was this unpredictable for everyone. If I gave my baby girl everything I had and still couldn't save her, perhaps others also gave everything they had and were similarly unable to alter the odds. Maddie gave me the greatest gift of all—she grew my empathy. She grew my heart.

I lost my innocence. I lost the ability to relax, to be the forever-positive and happy-go-lucky friend. Now when I hear someone is pregnant, my first thought is, "I hope the baby survives, I hope they get to meet their child." That never occurred to me before. I am aware in a way I never was before that a dark side of the world exists, and that no one is immune to it. When I see people who have the privilege of being forever-positive, I feel a flash of sadness for who I was, and yes, even a flash of envy that they are afforded that privilege. How lovely to be allowed to go through life without the deep awareness that children die. How lovely to have the privilege of assuming the world will turn in your favor. I miss who I was sometimes. I miss her endless optimism. I miss her rose-tinted glasses. I miss her confidence. And mostly, I miss her happiness. I lost my innocence in a way that will never be able to be measured when I lost Maddie. I lost my faith in a happy ending.

And finally, I lost myself. I am not the person I was before Maddie's death, nor should I be. I was not able to survive her death. I became a different person. I became a more aware, more empathetic, more conscientious person. The person I was prior to her death no longer exists. The people who look for her will continually come up empty because she vanished with Maddie. I died the day Maddie died, and was reborn in her memory. I am continually struggling to redefine who this new version of me is, and who I want her to be. Maddie gave me that. She changed me, just as Liam changed you. Whether our children live or not, they make us who we are. We see our reflections in our children's hearts, whether those hearts beat or have stilled.

Losing a child to stillbirth is an immeasurable tragedy. You are not who you were before. Your life has changed. Your son died. He has made you who you are, and you, you will live the rest of your life changing the world in his memory, whether consciously or not. The loss of a child is not just a singular event. It is a series of indescribable events. It is a series of indescribable losses. It is a story of indescribable survival. And, it is a story of indescribable love. I believe it is important to remind ourselves of the good our children have brought to the world. They have not only brought loss. They brought love. They brought empathy. They brought strength. They continue to grow our hearts daily. The world may never understand the depth of your loss, and that is lonely, and wrong, and unfair. I will listen to your heart, however. And you will listen to another grief-stricken mama's heart in the future. And this is how our children live. This is how our children make the world more beautiful. They inspire us to care for others. They grow the world in love.

With love for Liam,

Sarah

My second child, and only son, passed away in utero ten days before his due date. Kegan Christopher died on a cloudless, bright fall day, and was born in the crisp early hours of the morning. His labor was twelve hours long—twelve hours of knowing my son was dead inside me, twelve hours of believing I could love him back to life. Twelve hours of desperately trying to impart my own life into him with the strength of labor pains. Twelve hours. When he was born, there was no further question as to his life, no further denial of his death. Kegan was born perfect in all ways save one; he was devastatingly, breathlessly silent. My beautiful son was one of the approximately 23,000 babies stillborn in the U.S. every year.

Prior to Kegan's death and birth, I had only a cursory knowledge of grief. I had experienced death, but always a death I was warned of well in advance, and never the death of anyone in my intimate circle. I had never even experienced the death of a close friend, and certainly not the death of an immediate family member. My knowledge of grief was limited to what I had read in books or seen in movies; a period of intense sadness followed by "acceptance" and a return to the joys of your pre-mourning life. I had an image in my head of what grief looked like—the solitary tear falling down the grieving widow's face as she stares out the rain-streaked window, or perhaps a solemn toast to a lost friend in a boisterous pub, both followed rapidly by a return to laughter and light, by a return to normality. Nothing in my life prepared me for the soul-wrenching reality of burying part of your heart and then trying to carry on in their absence.

Before my son's death, I was not aware of how messy, long, and painful deep grief actually is. I knew nothing about how this level of pain manifests and was shocked to learn the reality firsthand. After losing Kegan, I was not the beautifully poetic griever I had always pictured, solemnly contemplating the world in her loved one's absence, and vowing to live every day to the fullest in his memory. Rather, I was the broken mother, loudly sobbing on the floor of her baby's nursery, surrounded by a pile of used tissues and forever unused baby clothes. I was the robotic mother, wordlessly feeding my two-year-old her snack while steadily avoiding eye contact to keep from breaking down into her yogurt and Cheerios—again. And, I was the anxious mother, constantly stealing away into my daughter's room at night to check that she was still breathing, to check that her heart had not stopped as well.

While I was grappling with learning the reality of how deep grief actually presents, I simultaneously found myself under enormous pressure to hide my newfound knowledge from the world. There is a huge compulsion put on the grieving to mourn appropriately, to stay strong and carry on, and, yes, to allow a small amount of sadness to peek through your facade, but certainly not enough to make anyone uncomfortable. A very clear message is sent that grief is expected, but only in small amounts, and only when it is socially acceptable. Your heart must be tempered both in intensity and timing.

At first, my husband and I tried to live up to society's expectations of grief. We certainly did not know how to navigate this new grief landscape, and if society told us there was a correct way to grieve, then surely, we reasoned, there must be a reason for it. We tried to show only a brave face to the external world, to not reveal the extent of wreckage in our hearts, and to turn the other cheek when friends and family members hurt us. We tried to grieve "correctly," as if by doing so we could give our son the legacy he deserved.

We rapidly discovered we could not survive this way, that the strain of grieving "correctly" was further diminishing our already tenuous ability to function in day-to-day life. I found any remaining sense of myself being slowly eroded by the constant pressure to grieve appropriately. We finally realized the best legacy we could give Kegan was not a false mirage of wellbeing, but instead an authentic representation of love. Grieving "correctly" does not necessarily equate to grieving well.

Grief is misunderstood in our society. It makes us uncomfortable, this reality that if you are so vulnerable, so am I. This realization that if your heart can break, mine can also shatter. So, we push it away. We pat the grieving on the back, send a casserole, and carefully avoid all mention of the dead in subsequent stilted conversations. When the dead are tentatively, carefully, tearfully brought up, we nod sadly before hurriedly injecting another topic into the conversation. We are trained from early on that grief isn't a pleasant, and therefore acceptable, emotion, and to consequently hurry ourselves away from its uncomfortable feelings. But...what if we embraced grief instead? What if we acknowledged the reality that we will all grieve, that we will all bury someone we love, and we learned to incorporate our grief instead of pathologizing it?

If we can't avoid grief, why not learn to understand it?

My husband, Karol, and I were shocked to discover both how multi-faceted and ever-present grief is. Prior to losing Kegan, we believed grief was restricted to the person who was lost. We had no idea how many internal mental schemas were disrupted by the grieving process. After Kegan's death, I felt completely lost in a world I no longer understood. I struggled with how to define myself, my family, and even a sense of security in the world. The entire world seemed unpredictable in a terrifying way I had never noticed before. It was as if I went to sleep and woke up in a parallel universe where up was down and down was sideways. Nothing made sense. Even more confusing, the rest of the world carried on as if nothing had changed.

Slowly, painstakingly, Karol and I had to go through each aspect of our life and redefine it. What does our family look like? Are we a family of three or a family of four? Is the shape of our family a triangle or a square? It turns out, it's something between those, an indefinable shape, constantly being molded and stretched. Our family is composed of a mother, a father, our daughter (Keira), and the memory of our son. We are both three and four, simultaneously. And then, we had to define who we are and what our roles are: Am I a mother of two or a mother of one? I'm a mother of two, but...I'm only raising one...and she isn't an only child, but she's being raised as an only child, except she's also not, because we celebrate and remember her little brother constantly. We are forever struggling to define our lives, to lay out foundations we can build our future selves upon.

I further lost the illusion of control in my life. During both of my pregnancies, I was obsessively careful. I took it upon myself to be the Ideal Pregnant Woman, to give my children the best this world could offer from day one. They both had college accounts in utero, were sung and chatted to on a daily basis, and went for regular, well-hydrated walks. All baby and pregnancy items were thoroughly researched and were the safest on the market. No risks were taken, and no expenses were spared. We were going to be The Ideal Parents. It turns out, it didn't matter. You can be the safest parent on the planet and still bury your child.

The unfairness of Kegan's death destroyed my understanding of safety and order in the world. I was fanatically careful with both of my children's pregnancies, but with Kegan, I was even more cautious due to the abnormality of his umbilical cord. As aforementioned, Kegan was an isolated single umbilical artery (or iSUA) baby—his umbilical cord had only one artery instead of the usual two. This condition was classified as "Isolated" as it was not accompanied by any morphological or genetic abnormalities; his cord simply failed to develop two arteries. While we have since successfully lobbied to have pregnancy management guidelines for iSUA babies changed, at that time they were not considered to present an increased risk of stillbirth and were not recommended for additional monitoring. However, we were obsessively careful and, along with our doctor, decided to monitor Kegan's activity and growth through twice weekly non-stress tests and weekly ultrasounds beginning at 34 weeks. Three or four times weekly I would trek up to the doctor's office and watch my little boy dance to the tune of his own heartbeat. I was constantly at the hospital those last few weeks, constantly watching out for my son, and forever on the alert to keep him safe. It didn't matter. He still died. He died, and other, in my mind, "less careful" parents were allowed to bring their babies home and I knew nothing in the world would make sense to me ever again.

After Kegan's death I was thrown into a whirlwind of confusion. Why had he died? Why him? Why my baby? I did everything right, beyond right. Other parents took risks every day, and yet my baby was the unlucky 1 in

160 U.S. births that end in a stillbirth. It seemed unbelievably unfair. A reservoir of slow rage over his death began simmering in the back of my heart, rage that would rapidly flame to life when I witnessed the risks others took with their babies. I eventually had to embrace the reality that Kegan's death was simply unfair. My son's death to stillbirth wasn't a judgment or punishment for being a poor mother. It was simply unfair. I hated, and still hate, this conclusion. It flies in the face of one of my central, core beliefs—that my own care or caution can protect the people I love. It turns out, nothing guarantees safety. We can do our best to keep each other safe, we can decrease our risk profiles, we can greatly increase the chances that those we love will be safe, but we cannot guarantee it. Life is still, to a certain extent, stochastic.

I lost my understanding of my role as a mother. Who was I if my son died? Was I still his mother? What did it mean to be his mother and how could I parent my baby through a world he would never experience? I learned to look for moments to share him with the world. Brief moments where I could bring someone joy, close my eyes, and say to myself, that was for Kegan. That love was Kegan. I learned to treasure those who would readily talk about him and who would perform acts of kindness in his memory. There is nothing so precious to a grieving parent as those who keep their child's memory alive.

I constantly have to reevaluate who I am. Whatever happened to the laughing, optimistic girl I used to be? Whatever happened to the carefree girl who fervently believed in fairy tales and happy endings? She was replaced with a wiser, more solemn woman. Kegan's death and our subsequent grief changed who I fundamentally am. I learned how to set boundaries with those who don't honor my son, I learned how to fully appreciate those who do, and, most importantly, I learned how to rely upon myself in a way I hadn't been aware of before. I learned life isn't fair, that sometimes your heart doesn't mend, and that love and laughter can still exist even in this soul-shattering paradigm. I am continually rebuilding myself in my son's memory, continually shaping myself into the mother he and my daughter are both making of me.

Grief is unique to the griever. There is not a right or a best way to grieve. The world will constantly try to teach you how to grieve, but all you really need to do is survive. So do what works best for you. Others can walk beside you, but it turns out, only one person can ultimately walk the path of your loss. Share your story, share your baby, and share your love. We will all grieve someday. It helps to know we don't grieve alone. It helps to know there actually is no correct roadmap to grief—all there is, is everlasting love.

Journal Prompt:

What surprised you most about grief? Did you have any expectations or preconceived notions about the grieving process before the loss of your child? How has your understanding of grief changed or stayed the same? How have you incorporated grief into your everyday life and, importantly, how would you like grief and remembrance to manifest themselves in your future?

CHAPTER 2: ON MENTAL AND PHYSICAL HEALTH

"When you hear the words 'there is no heartbeat,' a trapdoor opens and you fall."

~Zoe Clark-Coates

Dear Sarah,

I have been searching for a grief therapist or counselor. While in the hospital, we were given a packet of information on stillbirth and noticed seeing a therapist was repeatedly recommended. We are trying to do everything "right," but it's so hard to figure out what next steps to take! I have never seen a formal therapist before and am very intimidated at the idea. We actually did ask for a grief therapist/counselor while in the hospital, but they didn't have anyone specifically designated for grief, they only had a hospital chaplain to offer pastoral care. It was not a pleasant or healing experience—the questions he asked made us feel more alone and isolated, and now I fear finding a therapist will have the same results. Additionally, the process of finding a therapist itself also just seems so overwhelming! There are questions about insurance, experience with grief, experience with stillbirth, whether David and I should attend together or separately, whether Lyra should see a therapist...it's all so much to figure out on top of just trying to function in everyday life. Everyone keeps asking what they can do to help—I wish someone would make a list of counselors for me, then help us call them and choose one! Or, they could volunteer to babysit Lyra every week so David and I can go to therapy. Everyone talks about how taking care of your mental health is so important, but practically, it feels completely overwhelming to find the time or resources to even begin to do that.

I don't know what to expect in therapy. Does the therapist lead the conversation? Do we? How does it work? Our brief experience with the hospital chaplain was so upsetting we asked him not to come back. He talked about how we would go on to have many more children, as if that would comfort us over the child we had lost. Even if we DO go on to have more children (and that is a big IF, something I can't even think about right now), they wouldn't be interchangeable with Liam. They would each be themselves, and any future children wouldn't erase the death of our son. The chaplain also asked a lot about the days right before Liam died and if I had noticed any warning signs. I didn't, I had no idea anything was wrong. It made me feel as if I should have known. As if I should have been aware of what was about to happen, and the fact that I wasn't meant I wasn't attuned to the needs of my child. Talking with him made us feel so much worse and alone...I had to wonder if he had ever offered comfort to parents of a stillborn child before or if this was his first experience with stillbirth at all. At any rate, his comments have made me nervous about pursuing future counseling and therapy; I can't bear to hear those same sentiments repeated again.

And yet...seeing a therapist is so strongly recommended, I have to wonder if we should at least try it. Did you and Paul see a therapist? Did you find it helpful? All the information from the hospital and that I have found online talks about how important it is, I just find it so overwhelming and intimidating. Would you mind telling me about your experience?

With trepidation,
Evelyn

Evelyn,

I am so glad the hospital recommended seeing a counselor! Paul and I began seeing a grief therapist immediately after Maddie's death and it was one of the best things we could have possibly done. It was so...liberating. We were finally able to talk to someone who really GOT it, who understood what we were going through and with whom we could be completely honest. I try not to offer direct advice, but I can honestly say seeing a grief therapist changed, and very possibly saved, my life. I always recommend that anyone who is grieving, regardless of who they have lost, travel the road of grief with a counselor at their side. I see them as a guide, someone you can turn to with questions, or just to help you feel a little less alone.

It sounds as if the process of finding a counselor and worry over leaving Lyra are what are causing you to hesitate. In terms of finding a counselor, did the hospital have any suggestions? I have also found that local baby loss groups sometimes keep lists of grief therapists available. I can reach out to a local group for you and ask if they have a list of recommended counselors with experience in stillbirth or grief, and if you like, I can also call and ask about insurance and availability. Would that be helpful? In terms of Lyra, can you make a standing date with a babysitter or friend for each week? I would absolutely volunteer if only I were there. Do you have a sitter you like, or if not, can I help you find one?

When Paul and I began seeing a counselor, I also had a lot of questions and worries, including whether we should go alone or together. We initially chose to see a grief therapist together, which I found hugely helpful for understanding what each other was experiencing, and frankly, for forcing us to have some discussions we may have avoided otherwise. I found the process of seeing a grief therapist together helped us turn towards, instead of away from, each other in our grief. As time has gone by, our grief process has ebbed and flowed; sometimes our grief feels in sync and sometimes it feels like we are in totally different places. At different points we have seen a counselor together, separately, or even not at all. It is all a process and there is no one "right" answer, but I will say we both have found the process of having a trained professional guide us through this incredibly intense, unique pain to be enormously helpful. I would love to help find a grief therapist who fits you and David.

I am so sorry to hear about the chaplain at the hospital. I have long believed that all hospitals should have a dedicated grief therapist on staff. Most hospital chaplains and medical staff do receive some grief therapy training, but it would be nice if there were someone available who specialized specifically in grief. It's so important for hospitals to be able to provide bereavement care for their patients, and I'm sorry this particular chaplain fell short. The words he spoke to you were hurtful and wrong, and you are right, they likely came from a place of ignorance regarding stillbirth (although I know knowing that doesn't make them hurt any *less!). Of course any future children wouldn't erase your pain over losing Liam. Of course not. Nothing ever could. Liam was a unique person, not a replaceable amorphous baby figure. A trained grief therapist will understand and honor this. Similarly, a trained grief therapist, especially one who has specialized in baby loss, would never ask such insensitive questions about the time period right before Liam died and would certainly never blame you. If and when you want to talk about the time period leading up to Liam's death, they will delicately explore this topic with you in a safe way. I also found discussions about the period leading up to Maddie's death very upsetting, and it took going through it with our therapist for Paul and I to both begin to process those days. As I said, someone who is trained in grief therapy should understand these things, but if you do have another counseling experience that makes you feel uncomfortable or judged, then by all means, switch to a different therapist. Your therapist will want you to be honest and comfortable with them, and if it's not a good match, it's completely normal to look for someone else!*

I'm glad the hospital recommends counseling for bereaved parents however, and can definitely take the first steps of finding a therapist in your area for you. I will reach out to a local baby loss group and send you a list of recommended therapists and their insurance. I'm so proud of you for being open to taking this first step towards protecting your mental health!

With pride,
Sarah

Sarah,

Thank you for the list of therapists you provided! We had our first session with our new grief therapist, and I couldn't believe how helpful I found it! David and I were finally able to tell our stories to a completely neutral, open audience. We were finally able to talk about how we experienced the days leading up to and following Liam's death in an unreservedly judgment-free zone. I hadn't realized how much I was censoring myself around friends and family until I was able to tell my story freely to an objective listener. It was hugely relieving to be able to speak honestly, without worrying about protecting anyone's feelings or fending off implied judgments or blame. The ability to say exactly what I felt without being corrected as to the "nice" or "correct" feeling was validating in a way I hadn't expected.

While our therapy session was hugely liberating, it was also very challenging. Our therapist didn't push us to discuss beyond what we felt comfortable disclosing, but revisiting the pain of that day was, well, exhausting. I want so badly to talk about Liam, but it's also hard to talk about his death. I'm stuck in a paradox, a situation where I want to talk about my son all the time and I also break when I disclose the details of losing him. Our therapist didn't seem surprised by this in the slightest, rather she seemed to expect it. She spoke at great length about necessary self-care AFTER therapy sessions (and here I thought the therapy session was the self-care!). She frequently referenced therapy as basic medical care and emphasized that self-care was how we then treated our minds and bodies to process our sessions. She recommended that we go for a walk or out for coffee together after our session to decompress and to come together again before going home to Lyra. It was a lovely idea, and while we were still emotionally exhausted when we got home, we were able to be present with Lyra in a way we wouldn't have been able to if we hadn't taken that extra time to process our session together.

We talked a lot about the goals of therapy and what we were hoping to gain from it. Truthfully, I hadn't thought at all about any goals! I don't seem to be able to do anything these days looking more than a day in advance (if even that); we didn't sign up for therapy with any grand goals in mind, we signed up because we didn't know what else to do! But it was helpful to hear myself verbalize what I hoped to gain out of therapy, because as I spoke words about our future, I realized I actually did want those things. It was also helpful to hear what David hopes to gain and to understand his needs and priorities. We are slowly beginning to create the shape of the life our future selves will occupy.

We talked a great deal about shock, depression, and anger. I am still in complete shock over Liam's death, I can't believe this is our life, I can't believe this is our reality. I live most days in disbelief, not understanding or comprehending that this is real. Occasionally the numbness wears off, and then I am plunged into complete, piercing, take-your-breath-away heartbreak. I can't bear the reality that we will have to bury our son. Our therapist talked about shock as being protective, helping us to survive these early days. I have to wonder how long the shock will last. I am almost afraid of it wearing off because the pain of losing Liam is so great. I prefer the dull emptiness of half-existence to having to face my heart being torn out again.

I haven't experienced any large surges of anger yet. Oh, I've been angered at hurtful comments people have said, but we have largely isolated ourselves since Liam's death and I haven't come in contact with the outside world much. My prevailing responses have been emptiness and heartbreak. Almost every article or internet post I have read about stillbirth mentions anger though, so I feel certain it is coming. I am still too numb and broken to feel anger yet, I just want my baby boy.

Numbly,
Evelyn

Dear Evelyn,

I'm so glad you had a positive first therapy experience. You are right, it is exhausting! Part of the work of therapy is meticulously going through emotionally charged memories, layer by layer, with the goal of one day being able to visit those memories without being completely flooded with pain and anxiety. I hope that doesn't sound dismissive or minimizing, of course the memories will always hold pain, the hope is to one day be able to visit them without being transported back to them, to observe them without drowning in them.

What many do not realize about stillbirth is that you have not only experienced the death of your child (which is already far beyond what any of us are or ever could be equipped to process), you have also gone through an extremely traumatic medical experience. The actual process of giving birth to a stillborn baby is itself incredibly traumatizing, and a large proportion of bereaved mothers will go on to develop post-traumatic stress disorder, in addition to the more widely acknowledged depression over the death of their child. Through the birthing process, we are forced to be unwilling participants in the last moments of our child's existence. We are forced, by the biology of the situation, to be active, bloody, participants in painfully bringing our children into this world for the sole purpose of burying them. It is shocking to me that PTSD among bereaved mothers has only recently begun to be investigated, understood, and treated.

Also frequently underacknowledged is the physical pain the mother goes through. When you give birth to a living child, everyone is quick to help care for you during your postpartum time period. When you give birth to a stillborn child, no one wants to acknowledge you gave birth. Postpartum mothers are left alone both to grieve and to physically heal from the trauma of childbirth. How are you physically healing in these early days? I am sure your milk has come in and you are in the process of trying to suppress it. One of the cruelest truths of giving birth to a deceased child—

your body doesn't realize your baby didn't survive. All your body knows is you gave birth to a baby, and it does its best to feed that baby. Your breasts become heavy with milk, and yet you have no child to feed...the emotional anguish of having milk and having no one to give it to is excruciating. In the early days of losing Maddie, I tried everything to suppress my milk. I walked around with ice packs stuffed into three layers of tight sports bras and when that failed, followed the advice of online baby loss groups and traded the ice packs out for layers of cold cabbage leaves. The heat from my engorged breasts half-cooked the cabbage, leaving its scent to trail in my wake as I sadly wandered from room to room. I can still see the shocked disdain on a visiting friend's face when I explained that no, I wasn't making a stew, I had cabbage stuffed in my sports bra and my breasts were cooking it. To this day, the smell of warm, cooked cabbage takes me back to that moment of shame, that moment that could have been a coming together of souls but instead was an ostracization of the physical reality of giving birth to a dead child.

Have you been to the doctor for postpartum checkups to monitor your physical health? I always worry about the physical health of bereaved mothers; it seems to slip through the cracks in the greater context of grief. Our society doesn't do well with talking about the realities of childbirth when the child lives and their birth is greeted with joy and celebration, we certainly don't physically care for mothers when their child does not survive. How is your body healing in these early days?

With concern,
Sarah

Sarah,

You are the first person who has asked about my physical health. It's as if the world forgot I labored for seventeen hours and gave birth to a full-term baby boy. Thank you so much for asking. Truthfully, the healing process has been hard. The hospital sent us home with a Sitz bath to help with vaginal tearing, and to help my stitches heal quicker. Even the process of using the Sitz bath is emotionally charged however—I keep thinking I shouldn't have to do this without having brought my baby boy home. When Lyra was born, I remember I was shocked at the amount of postpartum pain I experienced while torn tissue healed, but at least then I had my perfect little girl to cherish. Now I feel as if I have gone through all this pain, and for what? I didn't get to bring Liam home. He is at the morgue, my body is torn to shreds, and my heart is in pieces. The physical process of healing is a constant reminder of what I am missing, of who should be here. My breasts are full, hard, and hot with milk that I can't give away, that I can't even pump for fear of stimulating them to produce more milk. So, they ache with the pain of being overfilled, while my heart aches with the desire to give milk to Liam and the knowledge that I will never be able to. I have milk and no baby. My body has betrayed me yet again.

I also have not yet healed to the point of being able to work out or exercise. I have always worked out to relieve anxiety and am not sure what to do when my physical coping mechanisms are taken away from me. I am hoping I will soon be able to go for long walks, at least. My body is slowly returning to its pre-pregnancy state. On the one hand, continuing to look pregnant while knowing Liam is dead was incredibly triggering, but on the other, the return to my pre-pregnancy body seems to be erasing him, painting an image where the last nine months never happened. Where I was never pregnant at all. David is worried that I am returning to my pre-pregnancy body too rapidly. I have more or less stopped eating, and so I have to say, his fears may be accurate. I have no appetite. How can I? My son is dead. I know I must carry on for Lyra's sake however and try to force myself to eat whatever I can stomach. Thankfully David has been understanding and hasn't tried to force or guilt me into eating more. When others have commented on my eating it makes me want to throw my (admittedly untouched) plate at them! It just feels so controlling and demeaning. But it is important to us to still eat meals together as a family and just the process of sitting at the table with David and Lyra usually results in me eating at least a few bites—old habits die hard.

David and I have stopped drinking alcohol. I mean, I obviously stopped nine months ago! But David has now stopped as well, and I haven't started again. We want to try to get through this acute period in as healthy a manner as we can. It's hard enough without throwing alcohol into the mix! I know having a glass of wine might make me feel better in the moment, but...the benefit doesn't seem worth the risk in the long term. Neither of us have ever experienced anything of this magnitude (how could we?! What else is even close to the magnitude of losing a child?), and mixing an addictive substance into the equation doesn't seem helpful. So, we have sworn off alcohol, at least for now.

I'm so glad you mentioned the trauma of stillbirth. We spoke to our grief therapist about this briefly, and she also mentioned the high percentage of bereaved parents who go on to develop PTSD. As for me, I can't close my eyes without being transported back to that room. That moment when they told me his heart had stopped. At that moment, the floor fell away, and I have been struggling to find my feet ever since. I am constantly running away from that room, constantly trying to find myself anywhere else but in THAT room. It is always there, though. I can't escape it. But then, it is also the only place I can find Liam. And so, I constantly return.

In pain,
Evelyn

A 2018 *General Hospital Psychiatry* report on the trauma of stillbirth indicates that close to 40% of bereaved mothers will develop post-traumatic stress disorder (PTSD). This same study found approximately 30% of bereaved mothers will develop Major Depressive Disorder and that there is high comorbidity between the two groups. In other words, a large number of bereaved mothers are both deeply traumatized AND depressed. Great. Lucky us.

The very existence of research on the psychological state of bereaved parents underscores a crucial change in how stillbirth is being approached, however. We are beginning to recognize the enormous, long lasting, psychological toll stillbirth takes both on individuals and families. Stillbirth doesn't just result in a period of intense sadness followed by a return to our previous emotional and psychological states. The process of giving birth to, or witnessing the birth of, a deceased child is itself an incredibly traumatizing event.

Post-traumatic stress disorder is characterized by intrusive and disturbing thoughts, feelings, or emotions related to a traumatic event long after the event occurred. Those who suffer from PTSD may experience flashbacks or nightmares reliving the trauma, and may feel isolated, detached, or estranged from others. The traumatized individual may also experience cognitive disturbances, such as being unable to recall certain details or aspects of their trauma. PTSD frequently results in feelings of intense fear or anxiety, similar to levels experienced during the traumatizing event, as well as an enhanced startle response to benign stimuli. Those who experience PTSD may also exhibit avoidant behaviors, such as avoiding locations, people, or items that remind them of their trauma. The traumatized individual is in a constant state of heightened alert, continually scanning the horizon for danger.

The previously outlined list of common PTSD symptoms described me almost exactly following Kegan's death. I would fear falling asleep due to nightmares placing me back in the labor and delivery ward, I couldn't remember entire conversations we had had multiple times regarding Kegan's autopsy, I would jump a mile at the smallest noise or slightest touch, and I would drive thirty minutes out of my way to avoid the highway that went by the hospital where my son was born. I was very clearly traumatized but was too deep in my own depression to be able to see it.

Importantly, not everyone who experiences a traumatic event will go on to develop PTSD. *Risk factors* can increase the likelihood of developing PTSD and *resilience factors* can decrease this likelihood.

Risk factors for developing PTSD include:
- Being physically injured during the trauma
- Seeing a deceased body or seeing another person be injured
- A feeling of horror, helplessness, or extreme fear during the trauma
- Sudden, unexpected trauma or death
- Having little or no social support after the event
- Additional related stressors after the trauma (*e.g.*, death of a loved one, pain after an injury, or handling finances or logistics related to the traumatic event)
- A history of mental illness or substance/alcohol abuse

Resilience factors that make PTSD less likely include:
- Having a strong support network and seeking out their support
- A childhood fostered sense of safety/security
- A sense of meaning or purpose in life
- The belief that we have control over the outcome of our lives
- A tendency toward optimism

The development of PTSD isn't an exact science, and it should be emphasized that these are all merely factors in a far larger picture. However, when risk factors for PTSD are taken in the context of the stillbirth experience, it's almost unbelievable that the number of bereaved mothers experiencing PTSD isn't higher. Stillbirths are frequently sudden and unexpected, the mother is physically injured during the process, the parents see, hold, caress, and cry over the body of their dead child, there is an overwhelming feeling of horror and helplessness, little ongoing social support is offered, and there are a multitude of subsequent additional stressors in the form of funerals, bills, autopsies, doctor appointments, and packing up the child's nursery and belongings. The idea that at least some trauma symptoms wouldn't be experienced by bereaved parents seems hopelessly naive and dismissive of the reality of what stillbirth entails.

The trauma of stillbirth has long been underreported, and subsequently, undertreated. After Kegan's death, I had an overwhelming sense of guilt for any self-care, which in my mind, included reporting my own trauma symptoms. I had a sense that, as a grieving mother, every symptom I reported to my therapist should focus on my immense sadness over losing my son, and that my own trauma symptoms weren't important or worthy of mention. In my deep sadness and confusion, I even believed I deserved trauma for my great failing of being unable to keep my son alive. It was only through skilled, subtle questioning from my grief therapist that the trauma symptoms I was experiencing were able to be drawn into the light and examined. Further, it was only once my trauma symptoms had been named that I was able to discuss them with my husband, allowing them to become a point of commonality and support, instead of a crack, in our marriage.

Seeing a qualified, experienced grief therapist hugely influenced how my husband and I saw and understood our own grieving processes. Society at large tends to pathologize grief, but through the eyes of our counselor we were able to understand that grief is nothing more than a natural, expected reaction to love. We grieve because we love. The challenge comes in understanding all the myriad ways love and grief bubble over into your life, and it is here that a counselor is especially effective.

The work of grief was once explained to me as transforming emotionally charged memories into less intense, less reactive, memories. The idea isn't to suppress or never think of your loved one or your trauma, but rather to be able to integrate them into your mind in such a way as to allow painful memories to be present, without creating emotional flooding. Traumatic memories create their own neural pathways, and the more those pathways are reinforced, the stronger they become. This is described in the old neuroscience axiom "neurons that fire together, wire together." This idea, proposed by Donald Hebb and affectionately referred to as Hebb's Postulate, promotes the idea of neuroplasticity, that by repeatedly reinforcing specific neural pathways, we can strengthen them. This is where neuroplasticity becomes really interesting—neural rewiring goes both ways, and we can also rewire these specific pathways to be less triggering, less harmful, less painful. By working with a qualified grief counselor and through other methods such as journaling, support groups, and medication, when necessary (and under the supervision of a physician), we can rewire our own neural pathways *to promote healing*. It is for this reason that I always recommend bereaved parents see a grief counselor—in a very real, biological manner, we can take steps to make our own memories less likely to emotionally flood us. In a very real way, we can save ourselves from drowning.

The period immediately following a loved one's death is characterized by intense grief, and over time, that grief slowly becomes incorporated into the survivor's life. However, in 10-15% of the grieving population, feelings of grief instead intensify over time and the bereaved individual has an increasingly challenging time adapting to their loss. This was previously known as Complicated Grief Disorder (CGD) but was reclassified as Prolonged Grief Disorder (PGD) in the 2022 text revision to the Diagnostic and Statistical Manual of Mental Disorders (DSM-5-TR). PGD is characterized by prolonged, pervasive grief with persistent longing for and/or preoccupation with the deceased at least 12 months after their death, accompanied by at least three of the following symptoms: disbelief, intense emotional pain, feeling of identity confusion, avoidance of reminders of the loss, feelings of numbness, intense loneliness, and meaninglessness or difficulty engaging in ongoing life. After Kegan's death, every single one of these symptoms described me.

Being both a bereaved mother and a scientist, I have conflicting feelings on describing prolonged grief as a disorder. As a mother, I will grieve my son, and grieve him intensely, until the day that I die. As a scientist, I understand that the first step in treating patients is naming and classifying their symptoms. That is to say, referring to prolonged grief disorder is not meant to imply these grievers are themselves disordered or grieving "wrong." It is simply a way of classifying long-term symptoms that may pose a struggle in the bereaved's day-to-day life. Just as PTSD may be a natural reaction to an extremely traumatic experience, PGD may be a natural reaction to the sudden, unexpected death of your child. Here is where working with a therapist can again be incredibly helpful; therapists excel at identifying factors or triggers that prolong or complicate the grieving process.

The recent focus on the mental health of bereaved mothers is incredibly validating; however, there is still a significant aspect of the bereaved mother's health after stillbirth that is commonly ignored. Any discussion on the health of a mother who has endured stillbirth must also address her physical health. Mothers who gave birth to stillborn babies still went through childbirth; they are just as much postpartum as mothers who gave birth to live children. However, whereas the majority of postpartum mothers in the hospital will get to go home to sleepless nights of rocking and feeding a pink, wiggling infant, bereaved postpartum mothers will instead be forced to go home to sleepless nights of tears, silence, and impossibly painful, leaking breasts.

The emotional and physical pain of your milk coming in after losing your child is hard to convey to someone who has not experienced it. I tried everything to stop my milk from coming in that first week—ice packs, tight sports bras, cabbage leaves, drinking special teas…my milk still came in, and it came in fast. My body knew I had given birth to a term baby and was determined to do everything it could to keep him alive. I hated my body at that moment, hated that now, now it was trying to save him, when it had already failed so spectacularly. "Too little, too late," I thought bitterly, glaring at myself in the mirror while changing the ice packs on my aching breasts.

My postpartum appointment the week after losing Kegan was excruciating. Returning to the hospital, the scene of losing my baby, for my stitches to be examined was more than I could bear. I sobbed through the entire exam. On the way home, I waited uncomfortably in the car while my husband went into a pharmacy to buy a healing cream and a blowup donut for me to sit on. Karol, always an attentive husband, knew he couldn't heal the gash in my heart and so instead looked for anything he could do to ease my physical pain. He vigilantly watched the way I walked, sat, and lay in bed, and would silently make adjustments to relieve my agony.

I put my physical health on hold in those early days. Eating ceased beyond what was necessary to sustain life; I began having dizzy spells and cramps in my hands from lack of nutrients. It may have been a form of penance, a way of punishing myself for losing Kegan. It may have been the fog of grief clouding my awareness of what I needed to do to stay alive—eating was for the living after all, and hadn't I died with Kegan? Whatever the reason, those first weeks and months took a toll on my physical health. I was especially appreciative in those days of friends who didn't judge or comment on my health or appetite, but instead wordlessly made it easier for me to survive. Meals that showed up ready-made or favorite treats that appeared on our doorstep were received with a deep gratitude, a thankfulness for remembering we still had to feed our remaining living child. One friend asked for a grocery shopping list, and when I was unable to wrap my mind around making one, showed up on her own with a trunk full of her best guesses. I will forever have a deep love for those who physically helped us to survive those first weeks and months.

Early after losing Kegan, I could not live in a healthy way. Karol and I tried our best—we sought out counseling, we abstained from alcohol. We made purposeful decisions to try to go through grief in as healthy a manner as we could. I still was not able to live according to what society labeled as "healthy." I could not eat; I could not sleep without waking from nightmares. Some days, I struggled to get out of bed at all. I judged myself harshly for these things, which I internalized as my failure to grieve successfully. I wish someone had told me there is no way to grieve successfully. After losing your child, all you need to do is survive. You don't have to survive in a particularly beautiful, poetic way, you just need to survive. Seeing a counselor made survival easier, as did having ready-made meals from friends, and a husband who was exceptionally attentive to my physical needs. It is remarkably difficult to take care of your mental and physical health when you're not sure you want to survive, and here is where friends and family can help. By making seeing a counselor and eating easier, they made survival easier. By making survival easier, they made survival more likely.

Friends and family can make attending to your mental and physical health easier, but what if you don't have local friends and family? What then? Who can you turn to? I found online baby loss groups to be remarkably helpful in providing resources to make the process of attending to both my mental and physical needs easier. Through online baby loss groups, I was able to find an experienced grief therapist, and also found tips on physical postpartum care. It turns out, I wasn't as alone as I thought I was. It turns out, there were a multitude of women who not only understood my mental and physical struggles, but cared deeply about helping me through them. I may never meet the many women who helped guide me through the realities of baby loss, I may never be able to thank them, but I am here today partially because of them. We may feel desperately alone following the death of a child, but the truth is, we never really are. Sadly, there are far too many women who have experienced similar losses…and they are only too willing to guide and care for you, if you will let them.

Journal Prompt:

What are the main topics you would like to address with a therapist? What would your mental health goals for therapy be, and what steps can you take to move toward them? What are your biggest physical health challenges at the moment? Is there someone you can turn to for help with your biggest physical health challenges? Is there a service you could subscribe to that will assist with any of these challenges (*e.g.,* to assist with food delivery or meal preparation)?

CHAPTER 3: ON LOGISTICS AND PRACTICAL CONSIDERATIONS

"And they all said, 'I'm sorry for your loss,' as if you were someone who could ever be taken from me."

~Robert Brault

Dear Sarah,

I realized I have never sent you a picture of Liam. It is strange because I share his picture with anyone I can, I use any excuse to say "Look! He existed! My boy was real!" I'm not sure why I haven't sent pictures, but I am including some with this letter.

Our greatest gift after Liam passed was pictures. I'm not sure how many pictures you have of your sweet Maddie, I know it was a different time and we didn't all carry cameras around in our pockets. Did your hospital take any pictures of Maddie? Our hospital contacted a nonprofit to take photographs for us. It was an organization dedicated to memorializing babies lost to stillbirth and neonatal death—professional photographers would actually volunteer to come into the hospital room and take photos of you with your baby. When I first heard about it, I almost told them not to come—it sounded invasive to have a stranger in the room during our intimate moments with Liam. I'm so glad we had them come though! It wasn't an invasion at all! They were so respectful and just in awe of our beautiful boy. Sharing him with them was a gift and I am beyond grateful to have beautiful photos of our boy snuggled in our arms.

I don't think people truly understand what stillbirth is until they see pictures. They lump it into pregnancy loss or think you just stop being pregnant. Pictures help. They convey the loss, they convey the heartbreak, but mostly, they show your sweet baby. I showed an acquaintance (who had been sympathetic, but also seemed to think I was carrying on a bit much with my sadness) Liam's picture, and her entire face changed before she blurted out "Oh! You had a BABY." Yes, a baby. A real, honest to goodness, chubby, pinchable, squeezable, perfect baby. The pictures help. I'm so glad the hospital knew to ask photographers to come, because I was in such shock, I could barely fill out the death certificate.

I'm so proud of Liam and I love how adorable he looks in these pictures. Look at his chubby cheeks! Look at that cleft in his chin! And his curls! So many dark curls! He got those from David. Liam looked so similar to Lyra as a baby—just a perfect little one. Isn't he gorgeous? I just adore him. He's such a little sweetheart. I hope you enjoy these sweet pictures.

With pride,
Evelyn

Evelyn,

Thank you for sharing your sweet photographs! Liam is so beautiful! What a perfect little baby boy! He is just precious.

Sadly, I don't have many photos of Maddie. As you said, it was a different time, and there weren't organizations dedicated to preserving images of these sweet little ones. Sometimes nurses would snap quick photos of them, but there was nothing organized. All I have is a blurry Polaroid. I am heartsick over it but have to try to take comfort in the remembrances I do have. A lock of hair. Her perfect handprints and her footprints—ten little fingers and ten little toes. Almost twenty years later and I can still remember the feel of those little toes jamming themselves into my ribcage. We used to joke that she would play soccer and do karate...now I hear other mothers make the same jokes and my heart catches in my throat. If only... if only you are so lucky that she can.

You mentioned Liam's death certificate. Were you able to also obtain a certificate of birth? I'm not sure if you are aware, but many states have recently begun offering a Certificate of Birth Resulting in Stillbirth. It's a small but meaningful gesture from the state recognizing that you gave birth, that you had a baby. That your baby mattered. I know you are probably overwhelmed with logistics at this point in time (who knew there was so much red tape involved in burying someone you love?), but at *some point, you may want to look into getting a birth certificate for Liam. I found Maddie's death certificate to be incredibly traumatizing. It is one of the only things I have to remember her by, but I hate it. I hate that it exists. I hate that I have a death certificate for my daughter instead of her kindergarten graduation certificate, or her silly Girl Scout art projects, or ANYTHING that she would and should have produced in her life instead. I hate it. But, until recently, it was all I had. I recently applied for her Certificate of Birth Resulting in Stillbirth, and I can't tell you how validating it is to have her birth be acknowledged by the state. If you would like, I can send you information on how to apply for one for Liam. Are there any other logistics you are struggling with or that I can help you with?*

No one tells you that when you bury your child, when you are laboring to remember how to breathe, you also have a host of huge decisions to make. There are so many logistical and practical decisions—how and when to bury your child, how to memorialize them, when to pack up their nursery (and what to do with all their cute little baby outfits and toys!), what to do with their brand-new crib and car seat...it's all so overwhelming. After losing Maddie, I lost all confidence in my decision-making abilities, even for mundane tasks. Nothing seemed to matter anymore, and at the same time, I was constantly terrified of choosing "wrong" or "incorrectly." I remember staring at different flavors of instant oatmeal one morning, completely frozen with indecision, because after losing my daughter, I couldn't possibly be trusted to make any decision, no matter how small or inconsequential. I couldn't even choose between cinnamon and blueberry oatmeal in that state, how on Earth was I supposed to make irrevocable decisions about how to best memorialize my baby girl? I couldn't, and the weight of the decisions crushed me.

There are so many practical, logistical decisions involved in burying your child that no one acknowledges, whether because they don't think of them or they feel awkward mentioning them. It doesn't behoove the parents to ignore their practical struggles, however. I would love to help

> with any practical considerations, or at least hear about the different decisions you are making as you lay your gorgeous Liam to rest.
>
> Here for you,
> Sarah

> Sarah,
>
> We are approaching the date of Liam's memorial service. It seems odd that you and I have shared so many letters back and forth, and yet David and I haven't yet said our final goodbye to our boy. We have been grappling with his death while he is, in a sense, still here.
>
> The funeral home has given us a catalog of headstones. A catalog. As if I were picking out Tupperware or a new comforter. How on Earth am I supposed to choose his headstone? Parents aren't supposed to pick out their children's headstones. Children are supposed to pick their PARENTS' headstones. That is the order of life. This is backwards and upside down, and I find myself unable to flip through the catalog's clean, glossy pages. I can't choose and I shouldn't have to.
>
> I also had no idea how expensive memorial services were. Why would I, I suppose. I've never been in charge of planning a memorial before. It seems shallow and selfish to even think about money at a time like this, but we do have to make choices we can afford. My understanding is life insurance usually helps pay for many of the costs associated with burial, but of course Liam didn't have life insurance. And we didn't put money aside to pay for his funeral. We didn't plan on buying a burial plot. We didn't plan on buying a headstone. We didn't plan on organizing and paying for a memorial service. We planned on bringing Liam home in his brand-new car seat, to his cozy new bassinet, in his room packed full of

cuddly new toys and clothes. So why would we be financially prepared for planning his burial at all?

Still, plan it we must; his service will be held this weekend. We are looking into buying the plots around him as well so that when we die, we can all be buried next to each other. It seems so morbid to think of these things and yet...we must. Was Maddie buried or cremated? We went back and forth for a long while and ultimately chose burial, with a closed-casket service. I still can't decide if it was the right decision, however. Nothing is the right decision. I am choosing from two wrongs.

I have yet to decide what to do with his nursery. So far it is untouched. I can't bear to pack it up. When did you pack up Maddie's nursery and what did you do with all of her belongings? I love the idea of donating them to a family in need and yet...I can't give them up. And then, there is the angry, bitter whisper in the back of my mind— "If they were lucky enough to give birth to a living child, they are lucky enough." I know this isn't charitable, and try to squelch these feelings of envy, but they persist. I wish everyone who was lucky enough to give birth to a living child fully appreciated how fortunate they are, but then I suppose that isn't fair of me. I didn't fully appreciate how lucky I was that Lyra was born alive until I lost Liam.

In bewilderment,
Evelyn

Dearest Evelyn,

Oh sweet mama. You are right. You shouldn't have to plan his funeral. You should never ever have to choose how to memorialize your child. It is all so unspeakably unfair.

We ultimately didn't have a memorial service for Maddie, I just couldn't handle planning one. As you mentioned, it was too overwhelming. Everyone had opinions about how we should plan it, whether it should be religious or not, whether it should be open to friends or only extended family, even the music that should be provided. We finally decided that it was upsetting us more to navigate all the external pressures from extended family, and that Paul and I would celebrate Maddie's life alone.

We also did not purchase a burial plot or headstone—instead we opted to cremate Maddie. So, instead of flipping through catalogs of headstones, I flipped through catalogs of urns. It was so hard to choose the right one. I didn't want anything too cutesy, but I also wanted something that acknowledged her babyness, the fact that she was a child. I wanted something beautiful, sweet, innocent, and timeless, like her. I wanted something that said "Maddie," but in truth, I never got to know the intricacies of who Maddie was. Picking out her urn seemed to highlight how little I knew of her personality, how little chance her personality had to grow.

I completely understand your fear of making the "wrong" decision here. Again, there is no right or wrong answer. All there is, is your love for your child.

In terms of the nursery—again, there is no right or wrong way or time to decide how to move forward with it. We were renting the house we lived in when Maddie was born, so when we eventually moved, we were forced to pack her room. However, that move happened long after she passed. I wasn't able to pack up her room before then, and truthfully, there wasn't any rush. Some people see packing up your loved one's belongings as a symbolic gesture of "moving forward" and "getting on with your life," but I would venture none of those people have ever had to pack up their deceased child's room.

We kept Maddie's room untouched for a full two years after she passed, a sanctuary where I could sit, clutch her unused loveys, and feel close to her. Packing up her room when we moved was impossibly difficult. We weren't ready to pack it, but then, who could ever be ready for such a thing? At what point do you become ready to pack up your dead child's room? At what point do you become ready to remove the last remaining evidence of their physical presence? She will always be in our hearts and minds, but her room was evidence that she was more than that, she was more than our hopes and dreams. She was a baby. Our baby. Our daughter. And she had a room, a room filled with carefully folded clothes, bunny loveys waiting in her crib, a changing table, and toys lovingly stacked in a toy bin. She was real, and then she was gone, and nothing will ever change that.

The packing up of Maddie's room was especially difficult because it was our final act of parenting that had its origins in the time before her death. We knew that after we packed her room, everything to do with her from that time on would be done entirely in her memory. The original acts of arranging and decorating her room though, those were acts of parenting we had begun during her life. Those were acts of parenting begun in happiness and hope, and the overwhelming love and expectation of meeting your daughter. Afterwards, after we packed up her clothes, toys, and pacifiers, after we boxed away the physical evidence of her babyhood...we had nothing left to continue from the time before her death. Everything from there on out was preceded by broken hearts.

When we packed up Maddie's room, our hearts broke a little more. We weren't ready to pack up her room, we weren't ready to move her further from this world into our memories. But then, we aren't meant to be. So, we brought her memory boxes to our new house and created a table in *her honor. We graced her table with her urn and pictures and hung her sweet handprints above it. This isn't how we anticipated having our daughter present in our home. But it is all we have.*

So take your time, sweet mama. Pack, or don't, whenever you are ready. Store his tiny onesies or give them away. Or, you can always store them for now and give them away further down the line. You don't have to rush through the process of returning to a "normal" pre-Liam life. Everything will be post-Liam now, and that is beautiful in the same way that everything after Lyra's birth is post-Lyra. Our children define our worlds, whether they live or not.

In memoriam,
Sarah

The logistics of death. The logistics of burial. The logistics of packing up life after death. Before losing my son, I had no idea that death involved so many logistical decisions that had to be made immediately, right now, maybe yesterday, and usually while someone was handing you a pen to sign an irrevocable form.

After Kegan died, all I wanted to do was curl up in a ball, squeezing my eyes tight against the pain that radiated through every fiber of my being, and here I was being asked to sign death certificates, autopsy permissions, and to fill out page after page of insurance. It was more than I could comprehend. Didn't these people know my baby had died? Didn't they know none of their questions mattered? I would stare at them uncomprehendingly, glancing at my husband to translate their sentences before squeezing my eyes closed again.

I have a clear memory of standing in a hallway of the labor and delivery ward in the early stages of labor, being asked to fill out page after page of insurance before being admitted to our room. I felt a deep disdain for the woman seated behind her desk, forcing the pregnant woman in labor to stand and fill out forms to deliver her dead child. My husband was similarly shocked into silence at that moment. I couldn't help but wonder how they treated women who checked into the hospital during the late stages of labor. Were their babies told to wait in the womb until the paperwork could be filled out? I dully wondered if those mothers were allowed to sit.

Once we reached our room, there were more forms to be filled out. Forms for the morgue, forms for the funeral home, forms for the state, forms declaring over and over, death, he has died, your son has died, and you must bury him. You must bury him, but first, you must deliver him. Here is a neat form where you can choose his manner of burial, see, we even have boxes you can check. We have made it easy and neat and clean, and let's keep this a sterile process with crisp white forms and forget you are burying your baby.

My husband and I rifled through the folder of information brought to us, flipping through the papers without comprehension. It felt surreal, like this was someone else's experience, or an impossibly tragic movie. At any moment I expected the director to call "Cut!" and save me from the agony of this scene, but this wasn't a movie, it was our life, and decisions had to be made.

At our request, our hospital contacted Now I Lay Me Down to Sleep, an amazing nonprofit dedicated to remembrance photography of babies lost to stillbirth and neonatal death. We wanted pictures of our boy, of his button nose, the cleft in his chin, and his pinchable, chubby cheeks. We didn't want to risk forgetting a single detail of his perfection.

Our photographer arrived a few hours after Kegan's birth. He gently entered the room, snapped pictures of our gorgeous boy, sighed over his beauty, and then wordlessly left. I will never be able to thank Now I Lay Me Down to Sleep enough for their priceless gift. Thanks to their amazing generosity, we not only have professional quality photos of our beautiful boy, but we also have pictures of us with our son. We have pictures of us holding him, kissing him, crying over him…loving him. We have pictures that show he existed, and we were his family. We have pictures that show our heartbreak yes, but more importantly, we have pictures that show our love. We have a visual testimony of love for our boy, and there is no greater gift than that.

After learning of Kegan's death, I had no doubt I wanted Now I Lay Me Down to Sleep to visit, but I have spoken to other bereaved parents who expressed initial doubt as to their presence. Would it be morbid, they wondered, to take pictures with a dead baby? Would they feel self-conscious in front of a stranger? These are legitimate questions, and each family must decide for itself, but I will say I have yet to meet a family who regrets having photographs of their child. Remembrance photographers are trained to be as respectful and unobtrusive as possible, and many come with their own history of loss, further increasing their sensitivity to grieving parents. I will never be able to express the fullness of my gratitude for the images Now I Lay Me Down to Sleep provided. They gave me the gift of sharing my son with the world.

After our photographer left, the next decision was whether a post-mortem examination would be conducted on Kegan. Karol and I rapidly agreed that we needed an autopsy. I am a neuroscientist and he an engineer, and our scientific minds wouldn't allow any other option. We had to know what happened. We had to know why Kegan died. We had to know if any other children would be at risk, either in a future pregnancy or if there was a rogue gene floating through our family tree which Keira may have inherited as well. And I had to know if it was my fault. The autopsy decision was a straightforward one for us but filling out the form was not. My hands refused to fill in the words granting them permission to cut open my son's body. Shaking and slipping, my fingers eventually tamed the pen into forming letter-like shapes on the page. I handed the form over as quickly as I could.

The decision to bury or cremate Kegan required more discussion. Karol and I had both already crafted wills expressing our individual desires to be cremated, creating a natural inclination in that direction. I wondered how I would feel if we didn't have a plot for Kegan though, if we didn't have a gravestone where I could visit and talk to him. The decision was ultimately prompted by my need to protect my child—I was afraid he would be frightened in the dark. I was afraid he would be cold in the damp, unforgiving earth. I couldn't imagine leaving him alone, cold, and frightened in the ground. An irrational thought, yes, but perhaps you can forgive the heartbroken, confused mother for illogical thoughts. I couldn't comprehend that Kegan was dead. And to be truthful, to this day I still can't completely comprehend it, and I don't think I ever shall.

We finally decided on cremation. While I wanted a place to visit him, it was more important to me that we had a way to take him with us if we ever left the state of Washington. I couldn't bear the thought of losing my boy a second time, I couldn't bear to ever be at risk of leaving him behind. Together, Karol and I picked out a beautiful urn with deep blues, purples, and greens swirling around its edges. A baby turtle rested on top, looking hopefully at the horizon. During pregnancy, we had joked Kegan would be a surfer, and I had spent months picturing my teenage son joyfully darting in and out of the waves. A baby turtle seemed perfect for our surfer boy, a perpetual symbol of the wild joy that superseded his death.

Karol and I decided not to host a large funeral for Kegan. I knew that entertaining and organizing a large event was more than I could handle, and besides, the people who felt Kegan's loss the most strongly were already present in our house. The people who loved him the most didn't need to gather, they were already here. And then there was the part of me that was afraid our family or friends wouldn't come to a funeral, and we would be abandoned in our grief, as opposed to choosing to grieve in solitude. I sadly remembered those who had chosen to skip his baby shower and decided not to risk further hurt. We decided to limit ourselves to sharing remembrances with those who had loved him while he was alive.

When I left the hospital that sunny November day, clutching a box full of footprints and one shiny lock of dark baby hair to my heart instead of my son, I couldn't imagine how I would survive the night. I dreaded walking through our door without my boy, walking into the home that would never house him. As my husband helped my aching, bleeding, postpartum body into the car I stared straight ahead, determined not to look at the empty car seat in the back. We drove away from the hospital and left our baby behind.

For months prior to Kegan's birth, I had been joyfully preparing every inch of our home to welcome him. There wasn't a room in our house that didn't contain at least one object dedicated to our son—a highchair and bottles in the kitchen, a baby swing in the playroom, his bassinet in our room, and of course, baby toys and books spilling out of every cabinet. Testaments of love that became testaments of heartbreak and loss. While we were in the hospital, my cousin and his family watched Keira, and we asked them to put the larger baby items in the garage before we came home. I couldn't fathom looking at them. The night we returned home, my husband snuck out to the car and lovingly removed Kegan's car seat, adding it to the pile of items our son would never use. I didn't ask Karol to remove the car seat; I didn't have to. He had seen the pain in my eyes every time my gaze rested upon it. It was the same pain he felt, the indescribable agony of living after your heart has been torn out of your body.

We waited to pack up Kegan's nursery until we moved houses. There was no need to, and truthfully, what would be the rush? I faithfully kept it dusted and vacuumed for him, the parent in me needing to keep my son's room clean, just in case. Just in case what? He wasn't coming home. And yet...there was a deep need to keep his room perfect, as if by keeping his room pristine, I could show him the love he never got to feel. When we eventually moved houses, Karol and I packed up his nursery after Keira had gone to bed, sparing her the pain of seeing us break down amongst his onesies, tiny socks, and cloud-soft loveys. Previously, others had generously offered to pack up his nursery for us and I am grateful I had the self-awareness to turn down their offers. Maybe for some parents, such an offer would be welcome, but for us, this was a sacred duty. A solemn moment of packing up the remains of the life you promised your son, your daughter, your spouse, and yourself.

Having never expected our son to die, Karol and I didn't have a fund set aside for Kegan's autopsy, cremation, urn, potential funeral expenses, or our own grieving process. We were thankfully in a financial position where we were able to handle these unexpected costs, but many parents are not. It turns out, death is expensive. We later learned of organizations dedicated to helping bereaved parents with the unexpected costs of burying and grieving their children. We learned of two of these organizations, the TEARS Foundation and the BeliEve Foundation, after Kegan's death, and have been honored to direct other bereaved parents to them. The Star Legacy Foundation, an organization dedicated to stillbirth prevention and advocacy for families of stillbirth, similarly provides logistical assistance, advice, and support to bereaved parents. It was through the Star Legacy Foundation that we became aware of yet another logistical challenge associated with stillbirth—obtaining a birth certificate.

At the time of Kegan's death, stillborn babies in Washington were automatically issued a death certificate but were not granted any form of a birth certificate. As parents, we found this incredibly psychologically damaging. Our son was born. I carried him for nine months, labored twelve hours to deliver him, bled for weeks after his birth, and endured painful mastitis from suppressing the milk my body wanted to feed him— he was born. There was no argument around the physical, biological fact that a birth occurred. So why was a death certificate forced upon us, but nothing was offered to acknowledge his birth? If the state acknowledged his death, if the state required us to make arrangements for his burial, shouldn't they also acknowledge that the body we were burying was in fact born?

In 2018, Washington was one of only a handful of U.S. states that did not offer either a Certificate of Birth Resulting in Stillbirth (CBRS) or a Certificate of Stillbirth. In 2019, we decided to change that and began to investigate passing a state law (referred to as Kegan's Law by our friends and family) that would allow issuance of a CBRS. It was only a very short while after a fellow bereaved mother and I began contacting members of the Washington State Congress to ask for their support that the reality of what we were trying to accomplish set in. We were in over our heads and needed help. Luckily, the Star Legacy Foundation was happy to oblige. They connected us with the BeliEve Foundation, who generously offered to sponsor a lobbyist to advocate for our cause and guide us through the process of passing a bill into law.

Previous efforts to pass a bill allowing a stillbirth certificate in Washington had been blocked. To pass our bill and enable Kegan's Law to become reality, we needed to both understand why stillbirth certificates were seen as controversial and to assuage the fears of those who opposed them, so we reached out to pertinent special interest groups to discuss their concerns. It turns out, their anxiety was centered around the thought that legally acknowledging a stillborn baby had been born would somehow impinge upon reproductive rights. For this reason, it was imperative for us to meet with reproductive rights groups and the Washington Department of Health to work on the specific language in our bill. Together, we drafted a bill that was respectful of the reality of stillbirth, and also was very explicit in its inability to be used as a stepping-stone in future arguments over reproductive rights. A key piece of this legislation was the decision to link our CBRS bill to the already existing death certificate issued by the state. By linking our bill to an already established vital record, no rights or definitions in statute could be changed. The only possible outcome of our proposed bill was that a bereaved mother would be allowed to request a Certificate of Birth Resulting in Stillbirth, if she so desired.

The next two years were filled with meetings with state representatives, state senators, lobbyists, and other brave, bereaved parents. Side by side, we fought for our children, telling our stories over and over and over, testifying on the Senate floor, and then when the Coronavirus-19 pandemic hit, testifying over our computers. We were confronted with a wave of misinformation surrounding stillbirth and unexpectedly found ourselves in the positions of educators—educators on stillbirth, but also educators on grief. The first year, our bill did not pass. I was devastated, retreating to my office to stare at my notes, wondering how I could have let my perfect son down a second time. We forged on, and slowly, ever so slowly, our message began to trickle through.

After countless meetings, our CBRS bill eventually passed in 2021 with strong majority, bipartisan support. Through the steadfast work of our team of bereaved parents, our lobbyist, and the Washington community, we were able to convey to our legislators the enormous impact a certificate of birth would have on impacting the mental health of bereaved parents. Through our testimony, the Washington legislature came to understand the importance of acknowledgment and witnessing—acknowledging the truth that a birth occurred and standing witness to trauma. In the end, this is really what Kegan's Law was about—acknowledging pain, but even more so, witnessing love.

In 2022, the state of Washington joined the majority of its country in offering a stillbirth certificate. Of course, this creates just one more logistical choice for bereaved parents, one more form to fill out...but it is a form that acknowledges the truth of their story. It is a form that treats their history with the respect and dignity it deserves. It is a logistical decision that recognizes their right to have their child's birth be acknowledged.

Before losing Kegan, I had no idea death was associated with so many choices, so many logistical challenges. I had no idea of the fear that comes with making an unalterable practical choice you may later regret. I had no idea your decision making was expected to be at its peak when your heart was at its lowest. I had no idea.

Logistics. The logistics of memorializing the brief moments your child was granted. The logistics of cleaning up a life they never got to live.

Journal Prompt:

Reflect on the logistical challenges you have overcome. What are some of the choices you have made, and how have they impacted the memory of your child and your life after your child's death? Allow yourself grace as you reflect on these choices and acknowledge the extraordinary strength you have shown in making these decisions. When you find yourself struggling, remind yourself of what you have already accomplished. Are there any future decisions regarding your child that are causing you anxiety? What are some ways you can draw on the resilience you have already shown when making future decisions about your child?

CHAPTER 4: ON THE PREVENTABILITY OF STILLBIRTH

"Millions of families experience stillbirth, yet these deaths remain uncounted, unsupported, and the solutions understudied...Stillbirths have been neglected by the global public health community."

~The Lancet Series on Stillbirth, 2011

Dear Sarah,

We recently received Liam's autopsy results. I still can't believe I am writing those words. My son's name shouldn't be mentioned in the same sentence as the word "autopsy." There shouldn't be cause for an autopsy of an infant. And yet...there is. There is cause for his autopsy because he died, and we had to know why. We had to know if we could have prevented his death. We had to know if any potential future babies would be at risk. And we had to know if Lyra or any of her future babies would be at risk due to a rogue gene. We had to know. I had to know. I had to know if I could have saved him. I had to know if it was my fault that I lost him.

So, on that day, on that horrible, horrible day when we both met our boy and bid him goodbye, we signed paperwork permitting a "postmortem examination." Clinical terminology can make the unthinkable more palatable at times, but there is no getting around what either a postmortem or an autopsy is. We agreed to let them cut apart our baby boy's body to find out why he died. I still can't bear to think of it.

It took a long time to get his results. I'm not sure why—I'm not a pathologist. Maybe it always takes a long time. Maybe what they show in murder mystery TV shows is completely inaccurate, or maybe they just don't prioritize returning results for a stillborn infant. At any rate, they took their time getting the results back to us. I have been torturing poor David during this waiting time, constantly berating him with questions. We went out to eat the night before Liam died, was it the food? Was there something wrong with our meals? What if I had ordered something else, what if we had eaten in that night instead? No one had any stomach issues after eating out, but, still, I question it. Or I bring up that at one point during the night, I woke up lying slightly angled towards my back. I wasn't on my back (my pregnancy pillow wouldn't allow that) but I wasn't completely flat on my side either...was that it? Did I not roll completely back to my side in time? Was this why he died? At this question, David points out that a) I wasn't lying on my back, I was still on my side and b) Liam was moving entirely normally the next morning, so my position was wholly unrelated to his death. Logically, I know he's right and when I asked my doctor, she also reassured me they weren't related. And yet, I wonder...I always wonder, about everything. I constantly go back through every minute, every second of that day, forcing David to relive it with me over and over and over, searching for any minute, any second, when I could have saved my boy.

It has been utter hell waiting for Liam's autopsy results. I don't know how I haven't completely lost my sanity from the yearning, the NEED, to know how he died. The guilt of wondering if it was my failure. I don't know how our marriage has survived my incessant, brutal dissection of the hours before Liam's death, but somehow, miraculously, it has. I am so grateful for David's calm demeanor through this all, for his steadfast commitment to facing the truth of Liam's death together. We are lucky we were both in agreement in wanting an autopsy. A postmortem isn't one of those things you can each make concessions on; you must be in total agreement. There was no argument about whether to perform an autopsy, no convincing each other. Just a simple acknowledgment that we had to know. We had to proceed forward together.

Here I am, complaining how long it took to get the autopsy results, but I haven't told them to you. I still have a hard time verbalizing them, even to myself.

Liam's death was due to torsion, or twisting, of his umbilical cord. His cord had a twist in it, and somehow, a blood clot developed at the site of the twist. They think it formed shortly before his death as there was no sign of it on any previous scans, but it's hard to know. At any rate, the twist was too tight, the clot too large, and his oxygen supply was cut off. Within minutes of his brain being deprived of oxygen, he experienced brain damage and died. Within MINUTES. That part kills me. There wasn't even a chance to save him; his death was too rapid and there were no warning signs, in any case. All that could have saved him was preventing the clot in the first place. I asked the doctor if it hurt, if his death was painful, and she assured me it was not. She said he likely just felt very sleepy and took a nap. I am so grateful his death was peaceful. I wasn't able to look the idea of a painful death in the face. Any time I would think of his death, my mind would recoil at the thought that he may have suffered and rapidly skitter around it. It was destroying me to think he may have been in pain. And so, I am grateful. I am grateful his death was peaceful; I am grateful he didn't suffer. I am grateful. And yet. And yet...I still wonder...why did this happen? Why did his cord develop a twist in the first place?

Liam had an abnormally long umbilical cord. It was detected during his 20-week anatomy scan, but our doctor appeared only mildly concerned at the time. "This happens sometimes," she said. "It's not clear why. We'll keep an eye on it, but I wouldn't worry. Babies have long umbilical cords all the time."

I did worry though. Of course I did. We did extra monitoring of him because I was so worried. The extra monitoring didn't matter. He still died. We still lost him. How could we have saved him? We knew he had something "different" about his pregnancy, we knew it wasn't typical. Why couldn't we save him?

I thought I would feel less guilty after his autopsy. I suppose I do, in some ways. I know it wasn't my negligence that resulted in his death. I know I didn't miss a sign he was in distress or do anything to hurt him. But...his death was due to a condition we knew he had. Why didn't they save him?

In sadness,
Evelyn

Evelyn,

Your letter broke my heart. It is not your fault. You did everything you could for your son. You loved him, you were careful, you listened to your doctors, you even went in for extra monitoring. You did more than many would have done, to be honest. It is not your fault that he died. The medical system should have saved him. Better, more nuanced care should have been recommended for him. Truthfully, this may not be your physician's "fault" either. She was acting in accordance with medical guidelines. The change needs to be at the level of those guidelines.

Babies with abnormally long umbilical cords are at increased risk for cord knots, cord torsion, entanglement around the baby, and cord prolapse. We (meaning the U.S. medical system) don't have great guidelines for preventing any of these events, rather the advice seems to be to cross your fingers and hope they don't happen. We know abnormally long cords are associated with an increased risk of acute fatal accidents, but we don't take basic steps to prevent these accidents from happening. For example, cord imaging should be conducted on every umbilical cord during the standard 20-week anatomy scan. In cords with any type of abnormality, serial Doppler imaging should be performed to assess blood flow over time, and highly detailed cord imaging should be conducted to look for knots or twists throughout the duration of pregnancy. Knots or twists are hard to detect on imaging, and physicians disagree to the extent to which they can be seen, but repeated, detailed imaging of the entire length of the cord should still be done just to be thorough. Finally, it is my personal belief that if any umbilical cord abnormality is detected, the baby should be delivered as soon as they reach term (37 weeks). Once a woman reaches term, each subsequent week only increases her chance of stillbirth. If there is already a risk factor for stillbirth present, my personal opinion is get that baby out of there as soon as you can!

Our medical system doesn't provide adequate guidance for preventing acute accidents of these sorts. I say "our system," because other medical systems in the world have much lower rates of stillbirth. There are so many things we could do differently in the U.S. to prevent stillbirth, but for some reason, it doesn't seem to be a priority here. After I lost Maddie, I was told "it's just one of those things," and to just hope it wouldn't happen again. But here's the truth...it's NOT "just one of those things." Other countries have both lower rates of stillbirth and higher rates of DECREASING stillbirth. They are proof that stillbirth can be prevented, if only the medical system makes it a priority!

Maddie's death was also due to a cord accident. Her cord was pressed against the intrauterine wall and became compressed. It sounds as if the blockage through Liam's cord was very rapid, very acute. For Maddie, reduced flow of blood developed more slowly. I reported multiple times that I didn't feel as if she was moving enough but was sent home. Maddie also could have been saved if only the medical system had taken my concerns more seriously. I know our stories can't be that unique and have to wonder how many other deaths out there were preventable. How many stillborn babies could have been saved? And why weren't they?

In frustration,
Sarah

Sarah,

Your final questions haunt me. How many stillborn babies could have been saved? And why weren't they?

This is why we need to do autopsies. We have to find out how these babies are dying. We have to find out what we can do to prevent future babies from dying. And we have to ACT on that knowledge. Medical guidelines have to change, medical training has to change. Stillbirth isn't something we have to accept. Our babies didn't die for nothing. They created more knowledge that can save more babies in the future. We just have to make sure that knowledge creates change.

I am going to petition the medical boards to reevaluate management of abnormal umbilical cords. Liam's autopsy wasn't just for us. It was for all pregnant women, it was for all babies, it was for all OB/GYNs and midwives. His autopsy created knowledge, it created data that can influence change.

This is how he will live on. He will save others. And I am so proud of him.

With love,
Evelyn

It is estimated that 23,000 babies are stillborn every year in the United States. This equates to roughly seventy babies being stillborn every day. For context, approximately seventy elementary school children can fit on a school bus. The equivalent of a school bus of children are born dead in our country EVERY SINGLE DAY. For 365 days a year, the equivalent of a school bus of babies is sent to the morgue. For 365 days a year, the equivalent of a school bus of babies enters the world completely silent, breathtakingly still. For 365 days a year, the equivalent of a school bus of babies sends ripples out into society, leaving behind a tsunami of heartbroken mothers, fathers, sisters, brothers, grandparents, aunts, uncles, cousins, and friends. A school bus full of children. Three classes worth of kindergartners. Every day of the year.

Stillbirth is, unquestionably, a tragedy, but the question for me is, is it a preventable tragedy? Are stillbirths able to be anticipated? Are risk factors for stillbirth able to be identified? Is stillbirth "just one of those things," or can we prevent some stillbirths?

In 2011 and 2016, *The Lancet* medical journal published subsequent multi-part series on stillbirth in which they repeatedly emphasize both the degree to which stillbirth is understudied in medicine, and the devastating consequences of this dearth in research. In the U.S., there are more babies lost to stillbirth every year than to Sudden Infant Death Syndrome and prematurity combined, yet the issue of preventing stillbirth is not prioritized. Stillbirth continues to be brushed off, downplayed, and overlooked. *The Lancet* identified stigma, lack of awareness, and fatalism as major contributing factors to this blinded and silent approach. Talking and thinking about stillbirth makes people uncomfortable and they hold the (false) belief that there is nothing that can be done to prevent it anyway, so why bother trying?

The 2016 *Lancet* series lays out a multi-step plan for reducing stillbirth rates, beginning with obtaining an accurate understanding of stillbirth prevalence via perinatal mortality audits. Currently, official documentation of a stillbirth may or may not exist depending on where in the world the stillbirth occurred. Further complicating the matter, there is also not a universal definition of stillbirth. Stillbirth is uniformly acknowledged to be the result of a gestationally advanced, naturally occurring, intrauterine death (induced abortions do not result in a stillbirth), but there is disagreement on when during gestation the death and birth must occur. In the United States, the temporal cutoff is twenty completed gestational weeks—a naturally occurring loss that occurs prior to this is classified as a miscarriage. However, in the United Kingdom the cutoff is twenty-four completed gestational weeks and the World Health Organization uses a definition of twenty-eight completed weeks. It is hard to understand an issue if there isn't universal agreement on the basics of how it is defined and measured.

Standardized high quality perinatal mortality audits would measure the prevalence of stillbirth, and, importantly, could also translate into better quality of care. Perinatal mortality audits could go beyond just recording stillbirth rate—they could also define and investigate key maternal care performance indicators. By defining and measuring maternal care performance indicators, we can obtain a more thorough understanding of how quality of care, both during the antepartum (pregnancy) and intrapartum (labor and delivery) periods, impacts the rate of stillbirth. By both measuring the rate of stillbirth and performing a standardized quantifiable evaluation of maternal care, the medical system can begin to understand what translates into substandard quality of care, and what role this plays in stillbirth.

The Lancet also calls for increased access to postmortem examination, or autopsy, following a stillbirth. A survey conducted by the International Stillbirth Alliance found a quarter of parents who endured stillbirth were not offered an autopsy. These parents were offered no chance to evaluate why their child died, no chance to ease their guilt-ridden minds, no chance to understand risk in a future pregnancy. And, correspondingly, the medical community was offered no chance to understand why a full quarter of stillbirths occur. This same survey reported only a third of stillbirths are followed by an autopsy, indicating many parents will not opt to conduct an autopsy even if given the chance. This is due to a plethora of reasons including, but not limited to, religious beliefs, cost, or the assumption that an autopsy won't give adequate answers. Of the autopsies that are performed, only a quarter of them are conducted by or overseen by perinatal or pediatric pathologists. The vast majority of autopsies are not conducted by pathologists appropriately specialized to working with babies. In order to prevent future stillbirths, autopsies should be offered to all parents, and ideally, would be conducted by perinatal pathologists. If we are to decrease stillbirth, we must better quantify why stillbirth occurs.

Fatalism, the idea that nothing can be done to prevent stillbirth, was identified in *The Lancet* as a significant barrier to reducing stillbirth rates. Encouragingly, fatalism is sharply refuted by medical data. Stillbirth rates are markedly higher in low- and middle-income countries (LMICs) than they are in high-income countries (HICs), demonstrating the importance of access to high quality healthcare. Within HICs, stillbirth rates also vary substantially. The 2016 *Lancet Series* investigated stillbirth rates among 49 HICs, and notably, also measured each country's Annual Rate of Reduction (ARR) or the rate by which that country was decreasing stillbirth prevalence. The Nordic countries tended to show the lowest rates of stillbirth, and the U.S. and U.K. hovered in the middle of the pack. Disappointingly, the U.S. showed one of the lowest Annual Rates of Reductions—out of 49 countries we came in second to last at 48. Reducing stillbirth rates isn't a priority here, and the data bears that out.

In recent years, Scotland has emerged as a champion of stillbirth reduction. A 2017 study from the University of Leicester demonstrated that from 2013-2015, stillbirth rates fell by almost 8% across the U.K., with Scotland leading the way. The decreasing rate of stillbirth has been attributed to public health interventions focusing on stillbirth awareness, and to the identification and medical management of stillbirth risk factors. In 2013, the National Health Service: Scotland established the Maternal Care Quality Improvement Collaborative (MCQIC), with the goal of improving health outcomes for babies and mothers by focusing on both the perinatal and neonatal periods. The MCQIC focuses on preserving fetal wellness through growth, movement, and monitoring techniques and importantly, allows the care provider leeway in rapid medical intervention.

Public health interventions aimed at reducing stillbirth have largely focused on the behavior of the mother. Mothers are told that if they don't smoke, if they sleep on their side, and if they count their baby's kicks, their baby will be safe. The selective focus on the behavior of the mother has sadly resulted in an advertent culture of blaming her if a stillbirth occurs. Recent studies, however, demonstrate that care providers themselves are not adequately aware of the relative risks of different pregnancy conditions and scenarios. A 2015 survey by the International Stillbirth Alliance that asked care providers to select the top ten of twenty-three known risk factors associated with stillbirth found care providers consistently underestimated risk of advanced maternal age (over 35 years), *in vitro* fertilization, multiple gestations, and maternal obesity. It is hard to provide quality maternal care without a clear understanding of the factors that threaten a pregnancy.

Pregnancy care in the U.S. is further restricted by a regulation forbidding elective delivery before 39 weeks gestation. This regulation, known as the "39-week rule" was formally enacted by the American College of Obstetricians and Gynecologists in 2009. The 39-week rule restricts labor induction or cesarean section of a term baby during the 37th and 38th week gestational period unless an approved "indication" is present. Notably, at 37- and 38-weeks' gestation, a baby is no longer considered premature. At 37 weeks and 0 days gestation, a baby reaches term pregnancy; the baby is considered early-term at 37 and 38 weeks, and full-term at 39 weeks. The list of approved indications excepted to the 39-week rule is very limited and extremely precise, with little to no room for any medical interpretation by the care provider. This rule is strictly enforced by hospitals, insurance companies, and professional organizations; physicians who "break" the 39-week rule by inducing even a day early face the potential to lose their job, their insurance, or their medical license.

In the years following formal adoption of the 39-week rule, term stillbirth rates in the U.S. increased. Various physicians have formally challenged this rule in the years since its adoption based on increasing stillbirth rates, however their objections have largely been overruled. This is in part due to the argument that while term stillbirth increased after the 39-week rule was implemented, infant death in the first year may have decreased. The conclusion was that the babies lost to term stillbirth were balanced out by the babies who survived the first year. According to the 39-week rule, it is ethically and statistically acceptable for my son to have died at 38.5 weeks, because a different child may have survived their first year for completely unrelated reasons. I have problems with this argument on both a moral and logical level.

The idea that increased term stillbirth rates are balanced by decreased first year mortality data is flawed at the most basic level. There are a multitude of factors that influence whether a child survives the first year after their birth, including vaccination rates, vaccination protocols, car seat habits, safe baby sleep habits, hospital follow-up, anti-abuse training, breast-feeding rates, available insurance coverage for infants, etc. It is far too simplistic to state that survival past the first year is determined by only one factor (39-week delivery), which occurs prior to birth and also just so happens to increase rates of term stillbirth. It has also been put forward that delaying elective delivery to 39 weeks decreases time in the hospital after birth. This may very well be true, but I would easily choose an extra week in the hospital over sending my son to the morgue. The outcome of a potential few extra days in the hospital after a 37-week delivery is nowhere near the risk of my son's death.

The 39-week rule also does not take into account a multitude of pregnancy complications. Kegan's pregnancy was complicated by an umbilical cord anomaly; as previously described, he was an isolated single umbilical artery, or iSUA baby. The umbilical cord typically has one vein and two arteries, but for whatever reason, Kegan's cord formed with only one artery. We were advised that because Kegan's umbilical cord condition was "isolated", meaning there were no additional abnormalities detected, his pregnancy should be treated as standard as long as his size and movements were standard. Being a scientist, I researched iSUA pregnancies in-depth and found a world of conflicting case studies on this condition. Some doctors stated iSUA puts babies at moderately increased risk for stillbirth and recommended early-term delivery, others listed the condition as benign. I was reassured by the guidelines from the Society for Maternal-Fetal Medicine which emphasized the benign nature of iSUA, merely stating an additional ultrasound may be considered in the third trimester to check growth and provide maternal reassurance. However, as I both had a cautious physician and was already anxiety prone, we opted for additional monitoring beyond this recommendation. We wanted to be sure that not only was Kegan growing well, but that his heart and movements were healthy, and so, during the third trimester, I began going in for weekly ultrasounds and twice weekly non-stress tests. At one point, I remember fearfully asking my physician if I should deliver early and being robustly assured that early delivery was not recommended for iSUA babies, that even the extent of monitoring we were doing was well beyond what most doctors would do. In truth, I have evidence of this second statement—I went in at the 36-week mark complaining of pain and happened to see a separate doctor at my practice. When I recounted the extra monitoring we were doing, he laughed in my face and scoffed, "That is so not necessary. iSUA isn't dangerous." Two weeks later, Kegan was dead.

Kegan passed away at 38.5 weeks. His cause of death on his autopsy was listed as a "probable lethal torsion next to abdominal insertion" with "marked vascular distension and probably thrombus." In other words, his umbilical cord was twisted next to his belly button and a blood clot formed, cutting off his oxygen supply. I asked the doctor who delivered him if iSUA was to blame, and he (very slowly and deliberately) replied that while it's hard to know, cords with any type of anomaly are more likely to twist or knot. Kegan's cord was more likely to form a lethal twist than the typical baby's would have been due to his cord anomaly. I asked why we didn't see the twist earlier or see the clot forming and was told twists are very hard to detect on ultrasound and that clots can form within minutes. It was likely that his fatal blood clot formed on the day of his death and killed him within minutes of its forming. Blood clots in pregnancy are silent, rapid killers—there were no symptoms, no external bleeding, no pain, no alterations in movement. He simply closed his eyes, took a nap, and shattered our hearts.

Kegan, without a doubt, should have been delivered as soon as he reached early-term. If he had been delivered at 37 weeks, we would almost certainly have two happy children running through our halls instead of one lonely little girl and an urn in our bedroom. Kegan was not allowed to be delivered early due to the 39-week rule; iSUA wasn't on the list of predetermined indications and so early-term delivery was completely forbidden. Conflicting evidence around iSUA meant the formal guidelines around it were confusing and inconsistent. Had I been pregnant in a different country, Kegan may have been delivered as soon as he reached 37 weeks, but here, iSUA was downplayed and early-term delivery was not allowed. Until my dying day, I will believe that my son died because I was pregnant in the United States of America.

A 2020 study on the association between umbilical cord abnormalities and stillbirth found that approximately 20% of all stillbirths are associated with an umbilical cord abnormality. Of stillbirths occurring after 32 weeks of gestation, approximately 30% were associated with an umbilical cord abnormality. We have the data demonstrating that umbilical cord abnormalities put babies at increased risk of stillbirth, but by and large, physicians are still restricted from early-term induction in these cases. Simply having an umbilical cord abnormality that puts the baby at increased risk of an acute accident (such as a blood clot), is not enough to warrant early delivery, there must also be evidence of a chronic condition (such as growth restriction) for early-term delivery to be permitted. The problem with this logic is it ignores the increased risk of an acute cord accident due to umbilical cord abnormalities.

After Kegan's death, we contacted the Society for Maternal-Fetal Medicine to implore them to update their guidelines on iSUA babies. The previous guidelines had recommended against the need for additional testing in isolated SUA cases, stating "at most, a follow-up growth scan in the third trimester, at 30-32 weeks, might provide useful information and reassurance." Notably, we did far more monitoring than SMFM formally recommended, and we still lost Kegan. He was at increased risk for an acute fatal accident, and the only thing that would have prevented his death was preventing the acute event by early-term delivery. Thankfully, SMFM was very open to discussing updating its guidelines with us, and they now formally acknowledge iSUA increases risk of stillbirth and recommend increased monitoring of iSUA babies. Sadly, however, iSUA is still not listed as an accepted indicator for early-term delivery. Our little guy's death may save a future baby by allowing a chronic condition (such as growth restriction) to be detected, but under the current guidelines, he still would have died.

In the years following implementation of the 39-week rule, more indicators for early-term delivery have slowly been added. However, this list is still far too strict and precise. In cases where the baby is at increased risk of an acute accident, but a chronic condition has not developed, there is little the physician can do. Care is reduced to simply monitoring the baby and hoping a chronic cause for early-term delivery develops before an acute fatal accident occurs. As a mother and a scientist, I understand why the 39-week rule was originally implemented and applaud its goals. However, it is too severe, and its extreme stringency ultimately cripples the care provider. Because the 39-week rule is so strict and so precise, the physician has little leniency in the care they provide. They are restricted from evaluating each case on an individual, holistic basis in order to provide the highest quality of care.

Stillbirth is not inevitable. Stillbirth is not something we have to accept and simply hope we are able to dodge. Stillbirth is able to be quantified, understood, and, importantly, prevented. Countries that have prioritized reducing stillbirth rates have demonstrated time and again that change is possible, that stillbirth does not have to be our accepted reality. There are steps we can take to decrease stillbirth rates in our society: We can better measure stillbirth through perinatal mortality audits, we can improve standards of antepartum care, we can conduct autopsies to better understand cause of death, we can increase education (among the public and physicians) on risk factors, we can continue to research unidentified risk factors, we can empower physicians to make individualized care decisions, and we can allow early-term delivery for any baby at increased risk of acute fatal events. For too long, for too many babies, we have granted stillbirth access to our delivery rooms based on the false belief that we can't keep it out. We can keep it out. We can save our babies. All we have to do is look our medical system in the eye and demand change. Stillbirth is preventable, if we commit to advocating against it.

Journal Prompt:

Prior to your child's death, were the risks of stillbirth adequately conveyed to you? How has information regarding the cause of death of your child influenced your understanding and/or integration of their death? Grant yourself grace as you examine the circumstances surrounding your child's death and reflect on the steps you personally took to keep them safe. Remember that you were part of a team dedicated to your child's health and that their safety was not only your responsibility.

CHAPTER 5: ON SOCIAL SUPPORT AFTER STILLBIRTH

"Your heavy heart does not make you a burden."

~Liz Newman

Dear Sarah,

The last remaining family members that were here for Liam's memorial service recently left. I so appreciate them coming and would have been incredibly hurt if they hadn't come, but...at the same time...it was so hard to interact with them! Don't misunderstand me, I am beyond grateful they were here. I had one (close) family member tell me it wasn't convenient with his schedule and he couldn't make it, and I don't suppose I will ever speak to HIM again. Making time to come to Liam's memorial, to show love for him and us, means more to me than I can express. AND, I also wanted to scream and hide from interacting with them the entire time! I feel so guilty, as if I were not being gracious for their presence, or were in some way a bad hostess, but then...I was being a hostess for the event of my baby's memorial service! It's SO HARD to talk to anyone in a semi-normal way!

Despite the reason everyone was in town, no one seemed to want to talk about Liam. He made them all incredibly uncomfortable, and everyone seemed to prefer to talk about the weather or sports. On the few occasions when he was openly grieved, I found myself in the role of comforter. It was odd, to comfort others on the death of your son. To a certain extent, we felt like spectators to our own tragedy. It was painful to see the reflection of our own sadness in others, to feel responsible for being the cause of their sadness and consequently, to care for them.

I know I am being challenging—I want family members to show up for Liam, but don't know how to talk to them; I want others to grieve him, but I don't want to be responsible for comforting them. I feel lonely, but also long to be alone. I just don't know how to exist around anyone other than David anymore. All other relationships feel artificial and forced. I'm beginning to wonder if I'm irreparably broken.

In loneliness,
Evelyn

Dearest Evelyn,

You are not challenging. You are not broken. You are GRIEVING. The emotions you are describing are perfectly normal. Of course it is hard to be around others. AND, of course, you also simultaneously long to be supported and have your grief and love for your son validated. Both of those can be, and are, concurrently true. Of course they are. Of course.

I so wish the changing nature of interpersonal relationships as a result of death were more openly discussed in our society. The more I have spoken to grievers, and to grieving parents in particular, the more I have realized that no one passes through grief with their social network untouched. We all lose friends. We all lose family. And not just distant friends and family, we lose the people we thought would be with us until the end. I refer to them as the collateral losses of grief, the secondary relationship losses that follow the soul-wrenching death of your baby. And they hurt, these collateral losses. Some relationships you can walk away from with barely a backwards glance, but some of them...some of them cut you to the core.

It is perfectly normal to have a hard time interacting with others following any death, and especially such a sudden and traumatic death as you have experienced. Our society doesn't treat grief with the respect it deserves in general, and when you consider the highly unique pain associated with stillbirth...people just have no idea how to respond. I think a lot of it stems from fear—fear of experiencing a similar loss, fear of saying the wrong thing, or just fear of witnessing the intensity of another's pain. That isn't to excuse any awkwardness or dismissals of Liam, I just find it helpful to understand everyone is bringing their own history and fears to your interactions. I've learned that the hurtful responses I have received very rarely actually have anything to do with me.

I'm so glad your family was there for Liam's memorial, even if you did find interacting with them to be challenging. I know their physical presence in grieving your baby is priceless...even if it does force social interaction!

Honestly, Evelyn, I found social interaction to be very challenging for years after Maddie's death. You aren't doing anything wrong. You are grieving.

With tenderness,
Sarah

Dear Sarah,

Thank you for your understanding and insight into changing relationships. We are, sadly, already experiencing that. As I mentioned, we had a close family member who didn't come to Liam's memorial because it was inconvenient. When I mentioned to another family member how much this hurt me, I was told I was overreacting and being too sensitive. Too sensitive! I have to wonder; would they have said that if Liam had been an older child when he had died? Would there have been more overt grieving of his death and comfort in discussing him if he hadn't died shortly before his birth? I feel to a certain extent as if they don't see his death as tragic as it is because he never drew a breath and, moreover, they didn't know him.

It hurt so much to have my grief be reprimanded and judged, and truthfully, it made me angry as well. There were other comments at the funeral as well—family "coaching" us to not be sad because Liam wouldn't want us to be (how do they know what he would want? He was a baby; he would just want his mama to hold him) or telling us we had to be strong for Lyra (as if we needed more pressure as we try to guide her through the loss of her brother). Or even saying things such as "at least he was a baby, and you didn't know him yet." Generally speaking, any statement beginning with "at least" doesn't come across as empathetic or helpful at all...even if the intent was to help us see a silver lining (what silver lining is there when your baby dies?).

There were a multitude of hurtful comments, but then, I also know everyone was there because they loved us. I know they weren't trying to hurt us. It was so hard to navigate. I am beyond grateful for their love, but I also want to tell them their comments hurt me so they won't say them again in the future. I just find myself so hurt and conflicted.

With love,
Evelyn

Dearest Evelyn,

Ah yes, the "helpful" comments and suggestions that cut your heart open. I know them well. It is so astute of you to realize that people likely don't realize they are hurting you. You are right, your friends and family were there because they love you. AND, their comments also hurt you. Let me ask you this, if you hurt a friend accidentally, would you want to keep hurting them in the future? Or would you want them to tell you so you could stop hurting them? I know I would want to know if I were hurting someone so I could modify my behavior. It is ok to tell your friends and family that certain comments hurt you. I would try to be gentle in how you convey it (no one likes to be reprimanded!), but...your feelings have merit. And, generally speaking, those who love you will want to know if they hurt your feelings so they won't do it again.

I remember a few months after Maddie died, Paul and I were at a family reunion. All the grown siblings were present and grandchildren were crawling all over the place. I was already feeling uncomfortable being around so many "normal" people and seeing complete family units, when Paul's mother made a comment about all her grandchildren being present. Evelyn, it cut right through me. All her grandchildren. As if Maddie didn't count. As if she had never existed. Paul looked straight at me, saw my eyes filling with tears, and immediately said "well, not all the grandchildren. Not the youngest grandchild, not Maddie." The entire room was immediately filled with an incredibly awkward silence, but I was SO GRATEFUL to Paul. Never again did anyone refer to all the living grandchildren as "all the grandchildren." Paul's mother didn't maliciously leave out Maddie, I think she didn't know how to approach her. I think she wanted to be happy in that moment, and thinking of Maddie made her unhappy, so she just didn't think of her. And, painfully, I don't honestly know if Maddie IS held in the same place in any of our relatives' hearts as the other grandchildren. I can't know that. But I do know that when we expressed our wishes for Maddie to be included in the future, she was. Because when someone loves you, they don't keep doing or saying things that they know hurt you.

It is hard to feel confident expressing your needs, though. In the moment, it's all you can do to breathe, to even process a painful comment. How challenging to hear a hurtful comment or question, process it, try to give the benefit of the doubt that the speaker didn't mean to cause harm, come up with a response, and give helpful guidance all in the span of three seconds! It's impossible. I promise you, however, it will get easier. All social interaction will get easier. It takes time, and, unfortunately, practice, but slowly, you will begin to feel more comfortable around people again. There is nothing wrong with you. You are not too sensitive. You are loving your child.

With love,
Sarah

Dear Sarah,

Thank you for your validation. Talking and mingling is just so hard for me! Even benign, mundane conversations feel like a minefield. I was at the grocery store just yesterday and the clerk asked if Lyra was my only child. I didn't know what to say. She isn't, but also, she is my only living child. I didn't want to burden the clerk with my heartache, but I also didn't want to deny my son. I completely froze. Eventually I muttered, "uh-huh" under my breath and left, but oh! Lyra looked so confused and I have been so upset ever since! I feel like I let both my children down. I feel as if I didn't stand up for Liam, and as if I didn't do a good job of modeling remembering him for Lyra. I feel as if I have completely failed. Again.

Lyra will be starting in a new school soon and I am dreading all the "get-to-know-you" chitchat. I know conversations will cover everyone's number of children, and I just have no idea what to say or how to say it. I suppose I should plan it out ahead of time—our therapist tells us to practice short responses to hard questions so that we don't freeze in the moment. I also need to tell Lyra's teacher about Liam ahead of time in case any questions about siblings come up in the classroom. It is so unfair, this feeling that I have to prepare myself for simple, normal conversations. As if his death wasn't hard enough, now we have to figure out how to simply function in everyday conversations too?

How do you handle casual conversations that cover how many children you have? How on Earth do you respond? I'm so afraid of saying something wrong, I feel I have to have the perfect response every time, and I'm terrified of making a mistake.

In confusion,
Evelyn

Evelyn,

Sweet mama, if you had a friend who was going through this, would you expect them to have the ideal response to every comment or question? I understand your fear of making a mistake, and I'm here to tell you, you don't have to be perfect. It's ok to not know what to say. It's ok to flub a response. It's ok to change your mind on what you feel comfortable disclosing. Again, you don't have to be perfect. Please grant yourself the grace you would grant to a friend you love.

I also love your therapist's advice to come up with a prepared short statement to respond to questions or comments that give you anxiety. In terms of other parents asking how many children you have; you can simply say "she had a baby brother who died" or "she is our only living child." My experience is that they will usually move on at that point. If they don't, you can divulge what you like or change the topic.

In this day of social media, I have found that many new acquaintances of mine find out about Maddie simply from reading my social media posts. It is an unexpected benefit of social media—I am spared having to figure out when to tell them, and they are able to learn more about stillbirth before discussing it with me. Social media has been an incredibly helpful way for me to convey our thoughts and needs to our friends and family.

Figuring out social relationships after burying a child is so hard. I have observed that after this kind of loss, some people automatically have a response focused on you, some automatically have a response focused on themselves, and most are somewhere in between. I had some friends I drifted away from, who eventually I was able to reunite with years later. I had some friendships end permanently. And, I developed new relationships with other grieving individuals.

You are not who you were before burying Liam, so those who expect to relate to you as they did prior to his death will continually be confused.

There is a transition period in which friends and family not only are introduced to the new you, but also are introduced to the reality of how your family is now shaped, and how you need that reality to be acknowledged. I have found that gentle forthright guidance to friends and family is the most helpful for making it through that transition.

I truly believe that, generally speaking, our loved ones want to help us, sometimes they just don't know how. It's ok to request what you need; those who are able to hear you will gladly learn from you, and for those who aren't able to hear you, well, it is good for you to know who they are in order to protect your heart. After Maddie died, I was terrified of establishing boundaries around her memory and our grief. I was so afraid that the people I thought I needed in order to survive would let me down. And, it turns out, some of them did let me down. It also turns out, I didn't need them as much as I thought I did. I wanted them in my life, without a doubt, I wanted their support through my grief...but...it turns out I didn't NEED them. I could survive in their absence. Once I lost Maddie, I found out I could survive almost anything. But I also know realizing you CAN survive without someone doesn't make the sting and ache of losing them any easier. You still want to share your baby, your love, and your loss with them. You still grieve the loss of your friend.

After losing Maddie, I stopped thinking of people in my life as inherently good or bad. We are all good and bad constantly, we have the capacity for both and that's what makes relationships so challenging. Instead, I began thinking of people as emotionally safe or unsafe. Emotionally safe people were granted access to my heart. Emotionally unsafe people...well, I had to reevaluate what a safe relationship with them would look like. Because ultimately, that's all I wanted—to be surrounded by people who wouldn't do further damage to my already tattered heart.

With love,
Sarah

The derivation of the word grief is "to burden." This raises the question, who is being burdened? My husband and I most certainly bowed under the weight of Kegan's loss, the impossible weight of empty arms. And yet, we also felt as if our grief was a burden on those around us.

Following Kegan's death, we found ourselves surrounded by sympathy and, paradoxically, that we were also increasingly isolated. A circle of love and support rapidly engulfed us, yet nothing could break through to the intensity and depth of our son's loss. That grief was ours alone to bear.

In those first weeks after Kegan's death, a multitude of wonderful, gentle, empathetic souls reached out. We were bowled over, almost overwhelmed, by the pure love and generosity of concerned family and friends. This love, this graciousness, was the good kind of overwhelmed. It was the kind of overwhelmed that says, you are cared for. You are not forgotten. Your son matters. It was the kind of overwhelming love we needed to function from one day to the next.

We weren't able to respond in kind during those early days. We said our thank you's and retreated back into the dark recesses of our tortured hearts. We were afraid to detail the depths of blackness that had settled over our souls, unable even amongst ourselves to look at our new reality head on. When we did gain the courage to tentatively share the intensity of our despair and heartache, the unexpected response we received was almost visceral revulsion and, uniformly, fear. "We want to support you" it said, "but not up close. We can't look at this pain up close. Please keep that to yourself."

In truth, I do not blame those who veered away from confronting the depths of our pain. It's scary, this reality that if we are so vulnerable, they are as well. This truth that, if obsessively (almost neurotically) cautious parents could lose a child, then their children are at risk as well. It's terrifying to look at the severity of our suffering, to see how much torment can be inflicted upon a human heart. And it's maddening to realize they can't assuage it. They watched helplessly from the side, wanting desperately to alleviate our pain, but being unable to comprehend its depth.

Our support system reached out in whatever ways they could manage. Some sent restaurant gift cards, some sent physical food, some sent sweet memorabilia to commemorate our boy, and others donated to charities in his name. These friends and family reached out in the ways they were able, and I am desperately grateful for their love and support. The simple act of showing up, of signifying their presence brought immense comfort. And then there were those who merely paid lip service to sympathy before rapidly backing away— "we're here for you," they would say awkwardly, and then never mentioned our son again. Those relationships have since largely stagnated or been severed.

In our initial grief therapy session, our counselor repeatedly emphasized the impact that Kegan's death would have on our interpersonal relationships. She warned us we would lose friends and family members, and that we would also gain or grow closer to new friends. I will admit, I didn't fully believe or appreciate the severity of these changes at first. Our friends and family were uniformly supportive in the early days. The shock of Kegan's death washed over our social network like a tsunami, leaving behind a deep desire to help us pick up the pieces of our broken hearts. As time passed however, I began to see the truth of our therapist's warning. The fortress of love and support erected around us began to develop cracks, almost imperceptibly at first, and then rapidly widening.

We found ourselves the unwilling recipients of advice on grief from those who had never born the all-encompassing pain of burying their child. "Look on the bright side, move forward and don't dwell on him, you need to focus on the child you do have." These words ran like a refrain through our conversations, a constant suggestion from those around us to move past Kegan's death. To spare them from witnessing the torment of our hearts. But what bright side is there when a child dies? Why should we have to move even further away from him than we were already forced to by death? And how does the presence of one child in any way lessen the loss of another? We pushed back on these statements, on these assumptions and attempts to control our grief. We challenged the logic and empathy behind them and were met with anger. We met the anger head on and found that underneath it was frustration and fear.

Our grief, it turned out, didn't just reveal truths about us. It also revealed truths about those surrounding us. As inner fears, discomforts, and confusions came to light, our external relationships shifted. Some friends and family distanced themselves from us. Some acknowledged the ways they had hurt us, apologized, and asked how they could do better. And some pushed back with fury. Early on, I met that fury with an anger of my own, a bright hot rage that anyone would dare try to diminish our son or control our grief. As time passed, I adjusted my path. Rage wasn't helping me, and moreover, the energy it took to maintain was hurting my own family unit. I spent years bashing my heart into a wall, trying again and again to explain what we needed and why we had the right to request it until I finally realized I was wasting my effort. While it is vital to communicate your needs, after a point you have to recognize that some people, for whatever reason, can't hear you, and move on from them. I learned the art of taking a deep breath, communicating our thoughts, and then observing the response. I learned that not everyone should be granted access to our hearts or everyday lives. I learned that some relationships, even very old or intimate ones, ultimately cause more harm than good, and that those relationships could be reshaped into more distant, safer interactions, or, if necessary, even ended.

Before losing Kegan, Karol and I floated easily through our lives and friendships. We tried not to take slights personally, and thus generally avoided friction and anger. We are both naturally conflict-averse individuals, more likely to give the benefit of the doubt than assume malintent, and for the greater majority of our lives have been almost unnaturally happy. After Kegan died, all that changed. It is impossible not to take slights about your dead child personally, there is nothing more personal to a parent than their child. After Keira had been born, I realized one place I would draw definite boundaries was around her, and after

Kegan died, that extended to his memory as well. Neither Karol nor I were accustomed to establishing strong boundaries, but suddenly, we found ourselves navigating a minefield of subtle dismissals of our son or gentle reprimands of our grief.

We worked together with our grief therapist to establish where our boundaries lay and how to communicate them. We learned to recognize the anger that followed Kegan's dismissal as stemming from our deep sadness and feelings of helplessness over society's desire to forget him, and further learned how to address and manage that response. We made it clear that those who did not accept or acknowledge Kegan as a part of our family would not be welcome in our lives. We communicated that Kegan was every part as important as all the living children in our extended families and that we expected him to be honored that way. And, we established that unsolicited reprimands or "coaching" of our grief was paternalistic, ill-informed, and unwelcome. These boundaries took a great deal of time to develop, and we are in a constant state of having to enforce them.

Data indicates that a lack of sustained social support is a commonality following the loss of a child to stillbirth. A 2018 study conducted by Tommy's, a U.K.-based pregnancy loss research and advocacy group, found that after stillbirth, 9 out of 10 families reported feeling "isolated and alone." This study further reported that almost half of families who endured stillbirth stated family or friends had begun to avoid them entirely after the loss of their child, and that three-quarters of grieving families said their relationships with friends and family had been negatively affected. The data bears out what we anecdotally discovered—the vast majority of bereaved families indicate their intimate social relationships suffer following the death of their child.

The deterioration of social support following the death of a child is even more tragic when you take into account how incredibly important social support is to grieving families. Numerous studies indicate that the social environment of a grieving individual is a significant effector of grief outcomes, and this is especially well-documented in the cases of grieving parents. Parents in a supportive, non-judgmental, accepting environment do better on a variety of psychosocial factors years after their loss. While the entirety of the social support network is important, familial support is shown to have the greatest effect on grief outcomes. Studies evaluating the role of different sources of support following stillbirth found that support from family members had the greatest effect on levels of maternal depression and anxiety. Data further indicate that support from family and friends has a greater effect on long-term (fifteen-month post loss) than short-term (one- and six-month post-loss) grief outcomes and maternal distress. Sadly, many parents, even those who experience strong support immediately following their loss, experience diminishing support in the long-term.

As time passed, Karol and I both experienced a pulling back of social support, and at times even anger, directed at our persistent grief and insistence in honoring our son. Regular arguments began to flare up around conversations focused on Kegan's death and our requests to honor him. I would attempt again and again to explain our family's pain and grief and was continually met with the statements that we were overreacting or being too sensitive. Shortly before the one-year anniversary of Kegan's death, the strain of these interactions began to manifest upon my physical health. I developed heart palpitations, physical weakness, and recurring migraines in proximity to arguments centered on Kegan. A trip to the cardiologist resulted in my being fitted with a short-term heart monitor to evaluate cardiac arrhythmia. The advice I ultimately received from my cardiologist was the same that my therapist had issued—if someone is persistently hurting your health, either emotional or physical, you can (and should) reevaluate the role they play in your life.

Following the deterioration of social relationships, many parents can begin to second-guess and blame themselves. I began to wonder if I was, in fact, being too sensitive, if I was expecting too much, if I was grieving "wrong." As society increasingly corrected me, I began to doubt myself.

It was only due to the validating support of our grief therapist and other grieving parents that I was able to recognize that society as a whole gaslights grievers. The term "gaslighting" refers to a psychological phenomenon that can occur in emotionally manipulative relationships. In these interactions, the gaslighter manipulates, misrepresents, or minimizes the truth until the recipient begins to question their own reality and, in some cases, their sanity. While gaslighting is usually thought of as an intentional act, it can, and does, frequently occur unintentionally as well. I don't believe society consciously *means* to gaslight grievers; on the contrary, I think society as a whole desperately wants to help grievers. The disconnect arrives due to a profound misunderstanding of, and discomfort with, grief.

Society wants grievers to move past the sadness and longing of grief, both due to concern for the bereaved, and, importantly, due to their own fears. I have observed a pattern of supporting the bereaved up until a certain level of honesty around grief is reached, at which point an almost reflexive jerking back of support follows. The unintentionally conveyed message is, "I want to help, but I can't engage consistently at a deep level because I am so uncomfortable with the idea of anything this painful happening to me. I care for you, but it doesn't feel safe for me to comprehend this degree of emotional agony." I personally believe this is the subconscious reason behind a large part of society's gaslighting of the bereaved; the reality of deep grief is too painful to witness, so grievers are either told their grief isn't as intense as their personal experience leads them to believe ("you are too sensitive") or, they are told they are grieving incorrectly and are therefore themselves responsible for the pain they are feeling ("just look on the bright side"). Again, I don't believe this is ill-intentioned. It is a protective mechanism employed by support networks in the face of intense emotional suffering, coupled with genuine concern for the griever. Society wants to move the bereaved past grief as quickly as they can in order to escape these distressing feelings. However, the truth of the matter is that we can't move past grief, we can only move through it and learn how to carry it into our futures. Grief, like love, stays with you forever.

The 2011 and 2016 *Lancet* Stillbirth Series identified stigma as one of the largest obstacles to supporting bereaved parents. Stillbirth is hugely stigmatized in our culture—there is an implicit (false) assumption that the mother must have mismanaged her pregnancy and that, consequently, her child's death is at least partially her own fault. Further, there is a disbelief that the parents' grief can run as deep as it does due to the young age of the child. Bereaved parents commonly hear some iteration of the sentiment "at least you never knew them," raising the question of how old does a person have to be for you to be allowed to grieve them. I am not who I was at five, fifteen, twenty-five, or thirty-five years of age. Does that mean if I had died at those ages, my mother should not grieve me because she didn't fully know who I would later become? The logic is preposterous, but it is commonly applied to those who suffer stillbirth and neonatal death. Your child is your child, no matter their age, and you love them with your entire being.

The Lancet further identified that stigmatization frequently occurs via silencing. Bereaved parents commonly report being silenced by the society around them, either through direct suppression of conversations around their child, or by the more insidious ignoring or avoidance of the topic. Silencing is considered a social management tool in stigma that reinforces the relationship between the stigmatizer and the stigmatized, and, importantly, is not always consciously utilized. This last bit is especially important—I would hope support networks don't intend to silence bereaved parents, but it's crucial for them to take an honest look at themselves and realize they may be subconsciously silencing the bereaved. We can cause damage even when we don't mean to. Not all silencing is malicious, some is simply due to discomfort, however, all silencing results in further heartbreak and alienation of the already struggling bereaved parent.

In the current era, social media plays a large role in grieving. Social media can convey news of the death to more distant social relationships, can serve as a platform for the grieving parent to communicate with the world, and can connect grieving parents to each other. While we used phone and text conversations to communicate Kegan's death to our intimate social circles, we used social media to communicate his loss to our wider circles of more casual friends. The outpouring of sympathy and support we received through social media was hugely healing and provided a balm to our lonely souls. We have continued to use social media over the years to honor Kegan, to educate about stillbirth, and to educate about grief. Numerous friends have reached out privately to thank us for our social media posts or to tell us how learning more about our grief process helped them be more empathetic toward other grievers. In a very real way, social media has allowed Kegan's death to create a ripple effect in educating and creating a more empathetic society. However, by inviting the world into our hearts, we have also invited in the inevitable judgment and pain that accompanies social media use. Some have labeled our posts too intimate, too sad, or too cringe-inducing. Some roll their eyes and scroll past, and a few have even corrected our grief on public forums. Social media holds the potential for love, support, remembrance, and healing; however, it also holds the potential to greatly hurt the bereaved.

One of the largest roles that social media plays in grief is connecting grievers. After losing Kegan, I found a world of online baby loss support groups. There were groups dedicated to pregnancy loss, stillbirth, stillbirth due to umbilical cord abnormalities...any facet of Kegan's death we could think of had at least one social media group connected to it. In those first weeks, I rapidly joined group after group after group, longing to connect with anyone who could relate to the deep hole in my heart. I would scroll through the posts detailing autopsies, funerals, empty nurseries, social struggles, and finally feel validated and heard. I felt connected to a multitude of moms I would never meet, but with whom I shared this one great bond—we had buried our children. As time went by, I began to recognize a pattern of depression following time spent in these groups, or a feeling of being ambushed when a baby loss post would pop-up unexpectedly on my screen. I began muting some groups and completely leaving others. I recognized that while online support groups are very helpful for some parents, for me, at that particular point in my grief process, they had transitioned from helpful to harmful. This underlies the complexity of online support groups following stillbirth. Many are run by fellow grieving parents, not certified psychologists or grief therapists, and therefore vary a great deal from group to group. Some groups are more inclusive and empathetic, with strict rules around what can and cannot be posted, others adopt a more laissez-faire attitude toward monitoring content and interactions. Groups can be highly supportive or can be a breeding ground for comments that cut straight to your heart. Data on the effectiveness of online support groups bear out this unpredictability and studies evaluating their helpfulness have yielded mixed results. Some parents benefit greatly from them, some find them harmful, and some are ambivalent about them. It is hard to perform high-quality studies evaluating the usefulness of online support groups due to the extremely high variability in the groups themselves. The most that can be concluded at this point is that for some grieving parents, certain online support groups may be recommended, and for others, they may not be.

It was through an online support group that I was connected with another local grieving mother who has since become one of my closest friends. She had lost her daughter approximately twenty years before we lost Kegan and had become a "peer companion" to regional grieving parents. I first met her in person at a downtown coffee shop, desperately clutching pictures of Kegan to my chest as I shuffled uncertainly toward her through chatting coffee patrons. I was on guard at that meeting, not sure how to interact, not sure how much to reveal, and not sure how to share my heart. I needn't have worried. As the years have passed, she has become my mentor and guide through the pathway of grief, listening to me cry, becoming indignant on my behalf, accepting me without judgment, and forever loving both my son and my daughter. I honestly don't know who I would have become in the aftermath of Kegan's death without her. I was lucky. I was extremely fortunate to find another grieving mother with whom I meshed so well, and who was also willing to take me under her wing. There were other grieving parents I met with whom I didn't feel an immediate connection. We had the commonality of our children dying, but that was it. There is immense pressure for local grieving parents to find and bond with each other, but truthfully, sometimes the personalities just don't match. However, when they do, when you find a person who not only understands what it means to bury a child, but also understands YOU, hold onto them with all you have. They will be your lifeline through the storm of baby loss.

It was my mentor who first helped me navigate how to introduce the topic of Kegan in novel settings and casual conversations. I felt comfortable talking about Kegan with family, with both intimate and distant friends, and online, but I didn't know how to handle social interactions where the other person wasn't already aware of his existence. A well-meaning checkout clerk would look at Keira and casually ask "is she your only one?" and I would freeze. A mom at soccer practice would smilingly ask about her siblings, and I would choke on my words. I knew how to talk about Kegan among people who already knew about him, but the mental task of figuring out when to mention him among people who DIDN'T already know about him was exhausting. I asked my mentor and she said that while she doesn't have a hard and fast rule for answering the question of whether her living children had other siblings, her answer was usually guided by if she would see the other person again. If she would see them again (for example, if they were the parent of one of her children's friends), she would reply "yes, she had a sister who died" and if she wouldn't, she may just shake her head and change the topic. However, she emphasized that the important thing was granting yourself grace in the moment and answering with whatever felt best to you and *was in line with what you could handle at that moment.* In other words, I didn't have to get it perfect every time. I could stumble through the answer, and it wouldn't mean I was betraying my son. As time has passed, I have gotten more and more comfortable answering casual questions about Keira's siblinghood with the truth that she had a baby brother who died. Sometimes I add in that he died shortly before birth, sometimes I restrict myself to a short, simple sentence of his existence. I do what I feel I have the strength for in that moment, recognizing none of these answers are betraying, denying, or letting down my son.

As time has passed, I have become more confident including Kegan in regular social interactions. I have learned to embrace those who are not made uncomfortable by him, and to look past those who are. I have learned to draw strong boundaries around his memory and to fiercely protect our family's right to grieve. I have said goodbye to friends who hurt our hearts and made new friends who bring us peace. I have taken distance from relationships and then have come back to them when they changed shape. I have learned to especially appreciate those who are willing to listen to our input and alter their perspectives on baby loss and grief. I have learned society in general doesn't know how to handle grief, but we can teach them. I have learned society wants to help. People want to help. They may not know how, and they may not get it right, but overall, I still believe the world just wants your heart to heal.

Journal Prompt:

Reflect on the impact your child's death has had on your social relationships. How has your social network altered since their death? Think back on ways individuals have supported you, and outline reasons you are grateful for that support. After reflecting on reasons for gratitude, consider the social struggles you have experienced related to the death of your child. Can you brainstorm statements or guidance you could provide to make those struggles less likely to occur again in the future? Contemplate what "safe" social interactions around your child look like to you and how you would like them and your grief to be honored among friends and family members.

CHAPTER 6: ON ROMANTIC RELATIONSHIPS AFTER STILLBIRTH

"What an awful thing then, being there in our house together with our daughter gone, trying to be equal to so many sudden orders of sorrow, any one of which alone would have wrenched us from our fragile orbits around each other."

~Paul Harding

Dear Sarah,

David and I have been fighting more and more frequently recently. I'm not sure what is going on, and I'm not even sure what we are fighting about. In the immediate aftermath of Liam's death, we pulled together and were such a strong unit, but as time passes it feels as if that closeness is slipping away. We were so united up until we buried Liam, but now, now that we have left the immediate logistics of death behind and have to figure out everyday life...we are falling apart.

We are completely out of sync when it comes to Liam. David is burying himself in his work, throwing himself into spreadsheets and memos as if our son never existed. I constantly want to talk about Liam, and not talk to just anyone, I want to talk to DAVID about Liam. I want to talk to the only other person in the world who loved my little boy as much as I did, and he's unwilling to do it. He goes straight from work to working out to bed, taking short breaks to interface with Lyra but avoiding being alone with me at all costs. I feel so abandoned by him; I just want my husband back. He was my best friend, now I feel as if I don't have a friend in the world. I feel as if I failed as Liam's mother, and now I am failing as David's wife. Our marriage, always so stable, suddenly feels impossibly fragile. I can't begin to see how we will survive this.

In loneliness,
Evelyn

Dearest Evelyn,

I am so sorry this is happening. I know it doesn't make it any easier to handle, but I hope it can bring you some relief to know it is very common for grieving parents to find themselves out of sync with each other. The two of you aren't doing anything wrong or failing in any way, it is incredibly common for couples to have relationship struggles after the death of a child. It is not highly publicized, but statistics actually indicate that in the decade following stillbirth, couples are more likely to break up than to stay together. I know that is incredibly upsetting to read and I'm not telling you to scare you in any way! I just want you to be aware that the problems you are having are very common; you are not alone and you are not failing in your marriage.

Paul and I also went through a very rough patch after losing Maddie. Similar to you and David, it didn't happen immediately after Maddie's death. At first, we drew together, finding solace in the only other person who could understand us. It was returning to the stresses of everyday life that slowly began to create a wedge between us. Small annoyances or inconveniences that before we would have laughed off created huge rifts, fights would erupt over the smallest disagreements or perceived slights. We were in a constant state of alert after losing Maddie, terrified of further death, angry at our treatment by society, forever vigilant to the need to defend our baby's memory, and just overwhelmingly heartbroken. The stress of having so many intense emotions constantly flooding our system was more than we could take, more than anyone's body and mind could take. We began to break down around the edges, and the first place that became apparent was with each other.

Paul and I began to take each other for granted. We would hold it together in public, then come home and collapse from the strain of acting "normal" in our abnormal lives. Despite our best intentions, anger at the world began seeping out of us, finding an easy target in each other. After this had been going on for a few months I remember us sitting down one night, holding each other, and making a conscious decision to save our marriage. We made a plan that included seeing a marriage counselor on top of our grief therapist. I know seeing a marriage counselor can be taboo in our culture, but it was the best decision we could have made for our marriage. Our counselor helped us walk through the mismatched expectations we had of each other and helped us brainstorm problem-solving strategies. Moreover, she helped us realize that while we both still desperately loved each other, love wasn't enough. We were in such an extraordinary situation that we needed a plan to help combat the anger and confusion that was seeping into our marriage.

Have you and David considered seeing a relationship counselor? Even for just one session, it may be helpful.

With love,
Sarah

Dear Sarah,

Thank you for your wonderful advice! David and I spoke to our grief counselor about our increased arguments, and she also recommended a relationship counselor. She said we may or may not find the relationship counselor necessary in the long-term, but that we should try seeing him at least once, and was she ever right! It is a different kind of therapy from our grief counseling, with different goals and strategies. We have only seen him once, but already our relationship is on the path to healing.

A theme that has come up repeatedly, with both our counselors, is that David and I are having different experiences, but we each assume the other is having our own personal experience. We are unique people, with differing levels of support, differing levels of comfort in expressing grief, and differing grief styles. We have each been getting frustrated with each other because we assumed the other person knew what we were experiencing, because we assumed they were experiencing it too. The truth, however, is we are each having unique experiences of the same event. Realizing this has been huge for us both; just knowing that David's reality is not the same as mine has prompted me to give him grace and the benefit of the doubt more, and he has similarly been more patient with me. It is hard to integrate that we are not living identical realities, and sometimes we find ourselves slipping back into being easily angered and snapping at each other, but I am finding that focusing on our unique realities and perspectives has been hugely healing in our marriage.

I am realizing that David burying himself in his work isn't a personal rejection of me and my needs, it's just his own unique way of dealing with grief. He is in so much pain that he is seeking solace through distraction, by burying himself in something else. I, on the other hand, have a grief style that propels me to share my heart. David wants to be there for me, but he isn't sure how to best do that while also respecting his own grief style. We talked a lot about what each of us need, and how we can communicate and provide those needs for each other. Just realizing that David wasn't rejecting me and Liam was huge for me. We have made a plan moving forward and I feel so much more optimistic about the state of our marriage.

With hope,
Evelyn

Dear Evelyn,

I am so thrilled for you and David! When Paul and I were going through our rough patch, I remember being completely heartbroken and overwhelmed. I was barely able to function after burying my daughter, much less focus on keeping my marriage afloat. I counted on him to keep the marriage going, but of course, he was in just as much pain as I was. I was counting on him, he was counting on me, and neither of us were working on our marriage. It took time, multiple unhappy conversations, and dedication, but slowly we both began to give more grace and take better care of each other. We had to forgive each other for not always being exactly what the other person needed. That was hard, that forgiveness. To feel let down while you are at your absolute lowest by the person who is supposed to know and love you best is excruciatingly painful. We were able to do it only when we realized we were BOTH at our lowest. Neither of us were being the best versions of ourselves, nor should we expect each other to be.

It was very helpful to us to realize that we both had changed on a very fundamental level. Neither Paul nor I were who we were before burying Maddie. In a very real sense, we had to get to know each other over again. This took time, patience, and a deep curiosity in each other. We had to constantly remain curious about who the other person was, and not rely on our previous knowledge of who they had been. This level of curiosity may be what saved our marriage. By saying, "how was this experience for you, now in this moment?" instead of making assumptions about each other's intentions or goals, we were able to give each other the benefit of the doubt and avoid falling victim to fast, reactionary anger. Of course, we didn't (and still don't!) always get that right. Sometimes we make assumptions about each other, sometimes we aren't curious about each other's experience, sometimes we take our hurt at the world out on each other. We aren't perfect, but I think the thing that has helped us, and almost every successful relationship I have witnessed, is that we are constantly striving to be better. We don't expect perfection out of each other, but we do expect ourselves and each other to be constantly trying to make our marriage better and stronger. Sometimes I fall short, sometimes Paul does. We don't have to be in sync, we just have to be able to have faith in each other.

I am so relieved that you and David are on the path to healing your marriage. It is impossible for any couple to bury a child and emerge on the other side unscathed. Your marriage will obtain some scars as you each learn who you are and what each other needs. I don't think it's reasonable to expect any marriage not to gain some scars during its duration, and especially not a marriage that has undergone such an intense, transformational pain as child loss. Having scars doesn't mean your relationship is failing, it means you learned how to move your relationship forward through the pain that life provided. We are constantly learning from each other and constantly learning how to best love each other. In the end, I think that's all we can really strive for.

With love,
Sarah

The odds are stacked against couples who endure stillbirth. According to a 2010 study from the journal, *Pediatrics,* stillbirth increases the risk of a couple breaking up or divorcing by 40%. This study followed 3,707 married or cohabitating couples over ten years and a total of 7,770 pregnancies. During the ten-year timespan, couples who welcomed a living child into their home experienced a breakup rate close to 40%. Couples who suffered miscarriage experienced a breakup rate of close to 50%, with the greatest breakup risk occurring a year and a half to three years after their loss, and couples who endured stillbirth experienced a breakup rate of almost 60%, with that risk enduring an entire decade after the death of their child. Statistically, you are more likely to separate from your partner than stay with them in the ten years following a stillbirth.

As a bereaved mother who also deeply loves my husband, these numbers are terrifying. I remember first reading them in the hospital, feeling a sense of heaviness settle into the emptiness of my womb. Was I going to lose my husband on top of my child? I knew we had a strong relationship, but...slim odds had bested us once before. How could we survive when the odds were so strongly aligned against us this time?

The 2010 *Pediatrics* study highlights a theme common to child loss—two people going through the same event do not have the same experience, and will not react in the same manner. Even though Karol and I both lost the same child, to the same circumstances, in the same family structure, our experiences are unique. Some of these differences are due to the inherent biology of the situation—I carried our son for nine months before laboring and delivering his still, breathless body. Karol witnessed these events, but, other than offering support, he could not physically participate in my process of bearing a child. Some of the differences are due to culture—men are conditioned not to grieve as openly as women, and pregnancy loss is (incorrectly) largely seen as only affecting the mother. And some of the differences are due to the fact that we are individuals, who each have our own perspectives and coping mechanisms. We will experience the same event, and the grief that follows that event, in unique ways.

As I reflect on how Karol and I have each approached Kegan's death, the paradoxical nature of grieving simultaneously both as a joint parent unit and also as individuals is strikingly apparent. We grieve in tandem, but not as one. We are together and yet apart, united and still alone. Each person's unique grief is their own to bear, and our task as a couple becomes learning our partner's grief and seeking out how to support them through it. Furthermore, we are, in some ways, seeking to understand the grief of a stranger. I lost who I was before Kegan died, and similarly, Karol lost who he was. Neither of our personalities was able to sustain the loss of our child; our hearts were set on fire, shattered, and remade in his memory. We had to relearn both who we were and who each other was. We had to learn how to support this new stranger in grief, just as we were each concurrently struggling with our own grief.

Every couple and every heartbreak are unique and what helps one couple survive will not necessarily apply to another. We are four years post the loss of our son, still in the red zone as far as the 60% divorce rate is concerned, still learning our new reality, and learning each other's needs. I can share what has worked for us up to this point in our journey, and what I have learned from other couples who have successfully cleared the ten-year hurdle, however, just as grief is unique, the process of two people who love each other coming together in grief will also be unique.

First and foremost, appreciate each other. Notice what your partner does for you, and truly, deeply appreciate it. There is a shining moment burned into my memory from those dark hours in the hospital, a beacon of light I reach for when I feel alone. That moment, that beacon, is Karol standing up for me during labor. While you hear a lot about the wonderful healthcare providers who help parents through loss, you hear less about the providers who make loss worse, who shame or offer substandard care to bereaved parents. I was at the hospital through a shift change, and my second nurse, the one who was there when Kegan was born, was firmly of the supportive variety—a kind, empathetic woman, with tears streaming down her face as she lifted my dead son into my arms. My first nurse, however, the one who was there right after we discovered my son was dead, the one who was there during the majority of my labor, was of the other, unsupportive, variety. She offered no emotional assistance, disdainfully lectured us on our (apparently incorrect) sadness, and, when I requested medication for labor pains, refused to call the anesthesiologist to administer it. It was at this moment that my husband, my conflict-averse, perpetually patient husband, shone. He demanded to know why I couldn't have pain medication, if there was a medical reason why it should be withheld, and insisted the anesthesiologist be notified. At that moment, I was not able to advocate for myself. I needed help; I needed a champion. And he was there. He was there, and he fought for me when I couldn't fight for myself. Years later, the memory of his determination and indignation has not faded. When I find myself feeling disconnected from him, I can reach for that memory and remember how strong his love for me is. I can appreciate his fierce choice to fight for his wife and then choose to look for a way through our conflict.

Notice what you do for each other. Not all moments will be as dramatic as Karol demanding my medical needs be honored, but that doesn't make them any less important or heroic. Notice if one partner gets up with your living children when the other is having a hard day. Notice if one partner rearranges their schedule to allow the other time to themselves, to exercise, or to visit with friends. Notice if one partner picks up the slack around the house when the other is struggling. Notice. Notice, and then acknowledge. When we grieve, it is normal to turn inwards, so we must make an extra effort to acknowledge the good our partner does.

Respect your individuality. Couples will mourn both together and separately. Respect that the way you each choose to mourn will not be identical, and your timing may not be congruent. Be patient with each other's timing and try not to be resentful if one partner is having a relatively good day while the other is struggling. Early on, I interpreted our incongruent timing as a personal rejection both of our son and myself. If Karol was having a good day, I interpreted that as a statement on his attachment to his son, as a statement that he didn't miss Kegan, or was getting over his death and leaving him behind. Furthermore, I interpreted his good moods as a personal rejection of myself. As I had carried and birthed Kegan, in some ways he still seemed to be a part of me. He still seemed to be physically connected to me, and any perceived rejection of him was also understood as a rejection of myself and my sadness. Of course, Karol wasn't rejecting or moving past Kegan. He was just going through differently timed waves of grief, the waves we have since learned will be present all our lives. Sometimes the waves recede and you have a good day, sometimes they come crashing in and you drown. We had to learn to have faith in each other's love and each other's grief. After Kegan died, we had to relearn how to respect each other's individuality.

Find a grief therapist you are both comfortable confiding in, and schedule regular visits with them as soon as you can. A trained grief therapist or counselor can help you turn toward, instead of away from, each other in your grief. They will be able to anticipate some of the roadblocks you will encounter, and help you navigate them together. Our grief therapist taught us not only to express what we were feeling to each other, but perhaps even more importantly, how to really hear what each other expressed. Setting time aside to talk about Kegan and the challenges we were each facing was crucial; by having a weekly joint therapy appointment, Karol and I were forced to have deep conversations about our hearts and our needs on a regular basis. After every therapy session, we would then go out on a dinner date to focus on rebuilding the positive aspects of our relationship. By finishing our therapy nights on a lighter, love-filled note, Karol and I were able to connect with a level of emotional intimacy that didn't leave us exhausted, but instead rejuvenated our marriage and brought us closer together.

Support each other's needs and timescale as you return to physical intimacy. You may each have completely different approaches to sex and intimacy after losing your baby. Sex and babies are wrapped up in each other; you can't completely divorce one from the other. Except in cases of assisted reproductive technology, sex is where your baby came from, and so engaging in it may be triggering or anxiety-inducing for at least one parent. Parents who aren't ready to or don't wish to have another child may be afraid to engage in sexual relations for fear of getting pregnant again. Parents who desire to have another child as soon as possible may develop a goal-oriented, mechanical approach to sex, devoid of pleasure or emotional intimacy, which can also put pressure and strain on the relationship. Sex can also be physically painful for the bereaved mother, who may be healing from childbirth for an extended period of time. Pregnancy and childbirth change and injure the mother's body, and the intense stress and grief of losing a child may slow down her healing process. Talk to your partner about what you are each comfortable with, what makes you *un*comfortable (recognizing those needs may change in either direction), and find a way of expressing intimacy in each of your comfort zones. Snuggling, kissing, hugging, and just physically supporting each other through your mutual loss are helpful ways to rebuild intimacy and a feeling of safety with your partner.

Respect that you have different parenting roles and different societal expectations, and these will influence both how you grieve, and how you express that grief. There has been an increase in the number of studies investigating a bereaved mother's grief in the last two decades, but it is only much more recently that the topic of a bereaved father's grief has been specifically broached. Historically, studies indicated that paternal grief was less intense and of a shorter duration than maternal grief, however recent studies indicate that may not be the case. Instead, the intensity of each parent's grief may be comparable, and may be more related to the individuals in question and the quality of their unique relationship with the baby during pregnancy than with their gender. However, studies do indicate that mothers and fathers tend to have different grief "styles" in how they manifest their grief, which are important to recognize in supporting the bereaved parent.

Grief research indicates there may be generalizable differences in grief styles between men and women. While every person is unique and these conclusions are based on generalizable trends and averages (so they cannot be directly applied to individuals), these trends can provide insight into how men and women may react differently to grief, overall. Recent studies investigating the grief that results from pregnancy loss and neonatal death found that men tend to be more instrumental and women more intuitive in their grief. Practically, this means that men tend to be more action-focused and women more emotion-focused. Instrumental grief focuses on activities, distractions, and problem-solving approaches to processing loss. Intuitive grief includes outward displays of emotion, such as crying, talking about the loss, and seeking out community support. Notably, these studies do not in any way indicate that these gender differences are due to inherent biological causes. Gender differences in how grief is manifested are likely due to a variety of factors, including social expectations and conditioning.

Men may be conditioned by society to think of themselves as "helpers" to their wife's pregnancy, and by extension, "helpers" to her grief. Society at large does not acknowledge the intensity of a father's grief and relegates him to a supportive role. However, qualitative studies using grief intensity scales indicate the intensity of a father's grief may actually be worsened when society does not acknowledge his paternal grief or hinders his expression of that grief. Fathers deserve to both have their fatherhood, *and their grief after losing a child*, acknowledged and treated with respect, and data indicates that not acknowledging the reality of the father's experience can actually be harmful to him. It is not unreasonable to take the next step to wondering how disenfranchising one parent's grief may put extra strain on a marriage.

The lack of acknowledgment of a father's grief begins in the hospital and lasts long after the parents return home. While I was in labor with Kegan, our healthcare providers consistently ignored Karol. He wasn't the mother, so he wasn't part of the equation. He wasn't treated as if his child had just died. Finally, I spoke up and demanded that they include him in any words of comfort, that Kegan's death wasn't my loss alone, that he was both of our son. I will never forget the grateful look Karol shot me immediately afterward. When we returned home, the same pattern played out. Consistently, people would ask Karol how I was doing. No one thought to ask him how he was coping after his son died. No one thought to invite him out for a beer and to just sit with him while he mourned. The message he was given over and again was that his emotions weren't of consequence, that he had to be stoic for the good of his wife. That his role was strictly that of helper and he wasn't entitled to a paternal role. That he wasn't a father.

Mothers and fathers who have experienced pregnancy loss or neonatal death both uniformly score in the high grief range on grief severity scales. This emphasizes that regardless of whichever parent's pain is "higher," "worse," or more "intense" they are *both* in a significant amount of emotional pain and should be treated accordingly. A 2021 study from *BMC Pregnancy and Childbirth* specifically investigating fathers' grief indicates that paternal grief increases with advanced gestational age and is the highest in cases of stillbirth (followed by neonatal death, then miscarriage). This may be a reflection on this type of loss being disenfranchised (and parents consequently not receiving adequate support, which is associated with increased grief intensity), as well as the sudden nature of stillbirth. Parents (especially fathers) of stillborn babies are often not treated by society as bereaved parents, as opposed to parents who endure neonatal death, who may be offered more resources or support. Additionally, stillbirth tends to occur suddenly, with no chance to say goodbye to the baby or even realize there is a chance the baby may not survive, further exacerbating the parents' subsequent grief. However, it is important to emphasize that all types of loss investigated in this study show grief intensity scores in the high grief range. All bereaved parents should be treated with love, respect, and acknowledgment of their pain and parental role no matter what type of loss they experience, or what their specific parental role is. Disenfranchising a parent's grief is harmful to the parent as an individual, and furthermore, can also make them resentful of the support their partner receives, which may eventually be harmful to their romantic relationship.

Parents may also receive differing levels of support from their workplace, which can consequently stress their relationship. Women who endure stillbirth are usually required by the biology of the situation to inform their workplace that they gave birth. Their offices watched their pregnancies develop, and the mother will need to request time off to heal after childbirth. Consequently, bereaved mothers may be more likely to turn to close colleagues for support. Fathers, on the other hand, can more easily choose not to engage with their colleagues over their loss, and thus may not receive emotional support at the workplace. Interestingly, those men who don't report losing their child to stillbirth to their workplace often show higher levels of instrumental grief. This specific data point is hard to interpret, but is of interest due to differing bereavement leave policies for men and women after stillbirth. The father may be expected to report back to the office the day after his wife gives birth, leaving the mother to recover in the hospital alone. This incongruence between how the parents are treated can further drive a wedge between them, providing more societal credence to the idea that stillbirth is the mother's loss alone. The father may feel delegitimized and alone, the mother abandoned and alone. Both parents should feel comfortable reporting that they experienced the stillbirth of their child to their workplace and should be granted bereavement leave, and furthermore, they should be allowed a substantial amount of time to grieve together before returning to any societal obligations.

Studies utilizing qualitative grief scales indicate there are a multitude of factors that can influence parental grief after pregnancy loss and neonatal death. Low acknowledgment, low social support, and low levels of support from hospital staff are uniformly associated with increased grief scores, as would be expected. Low levels of marital satisfaction are also associated with increased levels of grief; again, this makes sense from the viewpoint that support and acknowledgment play a large role in grief severity. Bereaved parents with high levels of support from their partner may be better equipped to approach the pain of child loss, and may also have their parental role more regularly acknowledged by their partner. Each parent's quality of attachment and duration of attachment to the deceased child can also influence grief severity, although these associations are harder to define. It is crucial to recognize that parents will frequently not be perfectly aligned on many such influential factors; one parent may receive more support than another, or they may have had different quality relationships with the baby. These incongruencies can also stress a marriage, as not only will the parents be living separate realities, but it can also be hard for them to see and acknowledge that they are each having disparate experiences.

I started this section with the statement that more relationships will end following stillbirth than will survive. Therefore, I feel it is especially important to emphasize that if your romantic relationship does end, *that does not mean you failed and does not make you a failure.* It is impossible for someone who has never experienced the unique, excruciating pain of burying a child to understand how hard it is to merely survive afterward, much less keep your marriage flourishing. Some days your relationship may seem to just be limping by. Maybe one day it will end, maybe it will not. That is a topic for another book, but I want to emphasize that if your relationship does end, that does not mean you failed. It means you and your partner were put in an impossibly painful place by life, a place no one should ever have to figure out how to navigate, and may have found that your unique paths forward will diverge from each other. It may mean that you both changed on a very fundamental level and that you no longer fit together as well as you used to. It may mean that you can now move on from each other to heal in the manner you each uniquely need. It may mean you can both move forward independently in order to find light in your souls.

Lastly, I would like to end this chapter with an optimistic note. Romantic relationships are not guaranteed to end after stillbirth. A 60% breakup rate means 40% of relationships will stay together. Karol and I consistently work on our marriage. We have always made having a quality marriage a priority for us, not counting on luck or passion to stay together, but instead, choosing to sit down and discuss what does and doesn't work for us as a team. Our wedding bands have "choose love" engraved upon them, the words forever pressed against the underside of our fingers as a constant reminder to work through miscommunications, anger, and hurt feelings. This is our family motto, and it is what we strive for every day. I, so unlucky in so many ways, am beyond lucky in my husband. He has calmed my anxious mind and soothed my tortured soul. But he hasn't done that through happenstance—he has done it through me actively telling him what I need, him choosing to listen, and us both choosing to give each other the benefit of the doubt when anger sets in. Fortuitously, our core personalities still fit together. The new me and the new him are altered and yet the same, a slightly different puzzle from before, figuring out how we fit together. We are lucky we still fit, and we constantly do things to make this fit easier, to smooth out any rough edges that emerge between us. We approach our marriage like we approach our grief—we are two individuals, trying to learn each other well enough to be a team.

Journal Prompt:

Reflect on how your romantic relationship has altered since the loss of your child. How have you personally changed and how has your partner changed? If you could tell your partner two new truths about yourself since the death of your child, what would they be? If your partner could tell you two new truths about themselves, what do you think they would be? Has your style of communication with each other altered since your child died? Can you brainstorm an activity or time you can both commit to on a regular (weekly) basis to focus on each other?

CHAPTER 7: ON SIBLINGS OF THE STILLBORN INFANT

"Sometimes you miss them and sometimes you don't miss them. But no matter what, you love them. You just love them so much"

~Keira Hatzilias, age five
(on missing and loving her stillborn brother)

Dear Sarah,

I have been growing increasingly worried about the effect of Liam's death on Lyra. She's such a sweet, sensitive soul and I wonder how we can even begin to hope she will emerge from this unscathed. We have been doing our best to parent her through the loss of her brother, but truthfully, we are making it all up as we go. None of my pregnancy books included any advice on how to prepare your child for her infant brother's funeral. None of my online mommy groups offered guidance as to whether a toddler should see and hold her brother's dead body at the hospital. None of my parenting blogs had any advice for explaining why most babies get to come home, but not her little brother. We are winging it, and we won't see the results of our choices and actions for years to come. I am so terrified we will scar our little girl even more. How on Earth are we supposed to parent her through grief when we can barely face each day ourselves? I feel as if I am failing as a parent...again.

Struggling,
Evelyn

Dearest Evelyn,

Oh it breaks my heart to hear your worry for your little girl on top of your grief over losing your son. I can't tell you the best way for you to proceed with Lyra, but I can tell you that a parent who worries to this extent about the emotional well-being of their child cannot fail them. More than anything else, your daughter needs your love, and it is evident that she has that in abundance.

Children grieve their stillborn siblings, just as parents grieve their stillborn children. I have never understood why a child's grief is ignored by our society. We spend months preparing our children for their siblings, introducing them to the baby in Mommy's belly and letting them feel the baby roll and kick, and then society expects them to completely forget their brother or sister when they die. How unreasonable is that? The best I can figure out is that the world cannot handle the truth of a child's shattered heart, so they pretend the child's heart isn't shattered. Your Lyra is lucky she has parents who are so concerned about her emotional state, who are in tune with the storm of emotions she is processing.

I would love to hear more about your conversations with Lyra concerning her brother, and your plans to include him in her future. You've got this, Mama. Your little girl believes in you, and so do I.

With faith,
Sarah

Dearest Sarah,

Thank you for the vote of confidence! We haven't spoken much to friends and family regarding Lyra's emotional state (who needs more unsolicited parenting advice!), but I did have a friend tell me that any problems Lyra was having were probably due to her picking up on my own sadness. I felt like the worst parent in the world in that moment. I try to be happy around her! I try to engage and play with her. I try so hard to be everything she deserves, but I feel like I am drowning in my own sadness. I want to be the mother she deserves, but how can I be when I already lost her brother? I couldn't give her a living sibling, and there's just no coming back from that. I failed her.

David and I spoke to Lyra's pediatrician and our grief therapist about our concerns, and they were both incredibly reassuring. Both of them emphasized the importance of Lyra witnessing our mourning of Liam (in a controlled manner of course! We don't want to scare our little girl with the intensity of our grief). They said that by her witnessing our sadness, she would feel empowered to healthily express her own emotions, and moreover, she would recognize the importance of children to their parents. Our grief therapist had a particularly interesting point—if we don't let Lyra see we are sad over Liam's death, we are inadvertently sending the message that if she died, we wouldn't care. It's important for children to know that their parents treasure them and would mourn them, and it's important for them to know that sadness is an acceptable emotion. The key is in regulating the intensity of sadness around her, to make sure our conversations are appropriate to her emotional development.

I have come to the conclusion that it is important to grieve those we love not only for ourselves, but to show the living we would grieve them as well. Furthermore, it is important to model missing those we love to show the living they are allowed to miss them too.

After seeking guidance from our "grief professionals," David and I feel more confident in speaking to Lyra about Liam. She has always had questions about Liam's death (why wouldn't she?), especially in the beginning when we told her Liam had "passed away." I can now see she had no idea what that phrase even meant! We have since started using the words "died" and "death" and have explained in more detail that Liam's body stopped working. Lyra is a scientist at heart, she's a little engineer in the making. She understands when things break. She just doesn't understand when they can't be fixed. She understands his body broke, now we are working on her understanding that sometimes, things stay broken forever. That some things can't be fixed. And all we can do is remember. All we can do is hold onto our love.

It breaks my heart to see her grieve. I have read a great deal about how hard it is on grandparents to lose a child to stillbirth, because in addition to losing their grandchild, they also are forced to see their children in intense emotional pain, but I have read NOTHING about the pain of watching a young child grieve. I sat on our steps with my poor baby girl last week, rocking her tiny body in my arms while she sobbed "I wanted to bring home the baby! I wanted to play with him! I wanted Liam, I wanted the baby!" and my heart broke all over the place. My poor sweet daughter. My poor grieving little girl. Her pain is more than I can take, I wish I could take it on myself for her. My cheated, heartbroken munchkin...she just misses her brother.

We are trying so hard to incorporate Liam into the fabric of our everyday lives, while also honoring the special place that Lyra holds. We want to give her opportunities to create new (maybe positive? Or is that too much to dream?) memories associated with him. We have been doing acts of kindness in his name, and it is so sweet to see the actions she chooses to do in his memory. We are trying to give Lyra active ways to grieve, if she wants to. This is where it gets tricky, we want to give her opportunities to grieve, without pressuring her to feel whatever we are feeling. It is a hard line to walk, but thankfully David and I are comfortable being calibrated by each other. We both know our primary concern is the emotional well-being of our little girl.

I had a very hard conversation the other day regarding giving Lyra a living sibling. I was meeting with a new OB/GYN (it is too triggering to see the doctor who managed Liam's pregnancy), and she asked if I wanted to have another child. I told her I did not at this time, and she said "oh, just wait until Lyra starts asking for a sibling." Sarah, it was all I could do not to start sobbing on the spot. Lyra HAS a sibling. She does. He's dead, but he's still her sibling! The doctor went on to ask more about when we might "try again." Try again. I absolutely loathe that phraseology. As if I had a temporary setback and just needed to give it another try. As if another baby would erase the pain of losing Liam. Liam wasn't a replaceable, amorphous baby figure. He was a person. An individual. He was...Liam. Even if we do go on to have a third child, she or he would be exactly that, our third child. They would not replace Liam. Liam will always be our second. Babies aren't any more replaceable than school-aged children or grown adults. They are loved as themselves, as the individuals that they are.

With anger and sadness,
Evelyn

Dearest Evelyn,

It sounds like you are doing an amazing job guiding Lyra through grief. It is so important to recognize and validate the grief of a child, while also honoring their individuality and emotional development. Some days she may understand the reality of Liam's death better than others, some days she may miss him more than others. It's hard to remember how a child sees the world, but I think it's important to remember they DO see it, and they feel it as well. I'm proud of you for honoring her loss and giving her space to define what it means to her.

In terms of the doctor you saw, I am speechless. I cannot believe a medical professional would speak to a patient so callously. I hope you decided she will NOT be your OB/GYN in the future! No doctor should pressure a patient to make a decision to have another child, and they certainly shouldn't discount a deceased child! I am so sorry that was your experience. We haven't spoken at length about future children, as that is such a sensitive topic and not something anyone else should ever pressure you on. Our doctor advised us to wait to try to conceive again for 18 months after losing Maddie. He wanted to give us time to process our emotions and to not, even subconsciously, try to replace Maddie with a new baby. He told us, "Let's be honest, you are going to grieve Maddie forever and no new baby is ever going to take the pain away. SO if you do decide to have another baby, it will be with the reality that your first born is deceased." I loved him for that statement. I loved him for recognizing that babies are not interchangeable and for realizing we would mourn Maddie forever. We did, eventually, go on to have additional children, and we have also kept Maddie present in their lives.

As I see you search for ways to honor Lyra's grief, I am reminded of our own journey with our children. It was important to us that our subsequent children (we had a daughter and son after losing Maddie) not only knew they had a big sister, but were given opportunities to honor her. Our living daughter writes Maddie a letter every year on her birthday, and then burns it in the fireplace. When she was little, she would draw her pictures, but as she has aged, her letters have turned into multi-page correspondences. I have no idea what they say, but I imagine she is asking advice from the big sister she never knew. I have watched my living children learn to navigate the question of how many siblings they have and have tried to emphasize that there is no right answer, that they are free to respond with whatever they feel comfortable divulging in the moment. It is hard, this need to defend our deceased child's memory while also honoring the emotional needs of our living children. I am so encouraged to hear that you and David are able to lovingly calibrate each other in this respect.

I would like to conclude with one last thought. You don't have to know all the answers on guiding your child through grief. Other people will offer their opinion on this topic, but honestly, unless they are trained professionals, ignore them. I firmly believe that as long as you focus on respectful, loving, compassionate acts toward your living child, you cannot steer her wrong.

With love,
Sarah

Our daughter, Keira, was two and a half years old when Kegan died. We had carefully planned to have our children two and a half years apart, hoping they would be close enough in age to be friends, but far enough apart in grade level that they wouldn't compete. We had gone through all the typical baby books with her, walking her through the process of her little brother growing in Mama's tummy, to him being born, to how life would change after he came home from the hospital. She had joyfully participated in every social media post about him and told strangers constantly that she was already a big sister to the baby in Mama's belly. She helped decorate his nursery and carefully wrapped jungle animal puppets to welcome him home from the hospital. She was a big sister. She was ready.

And then...and then all of a sudden, he was gone. And we had to figure out what to tell her, and when, and HOW. No baby book prepared me for telling my daughter her infant brother had died. No baby book had a section on "how to coach your child through impenetrable, drowning grief and confusion." We were left to our own devices, blinded by overwhelming grief while simultaneously trying our hardest to rationally and compassionately parent our living child through her own grief. There was no rulebook, no guidance from the hospital even. We were left to wing it.

We opted not to have Keira meet Kegan in the hospital. The topic of whether living older siblings should meet their deceased little brother or sister is a contentious one, fraught with deeply held, extremely personal beliefs and convictions. As with most topics related to stillbirth, there is no right approach to this question. What is right for one family will not be right for another. We considered Keira's age, her personality, our onsite external familial support, and all the idiosyncrasies that made our specific situation unique to us and decided not to bring her to the hospital. Karol and I both felt strongly that the reality of seeing and holding her dead brother's cold body would create further trauma in our deeply feeling little girl and that we could work to create other opportunities for her to make positive memories of, and associations with, him. The false belief that we had only one chance to get this decision "right," that once he was cremated she could never again experience him, initially put immense pressure on us, but ultimately, we realized there were opportunities for her to make memories of him external to the hospital environment and made the decision that was best for our family. I stand firmly by the decision we made today, knowing it was best for our little girl and our singular family structure. With that said, I know it is not the right decision for everyone, and each family must make the decision that is best for their children, their situation, their hearts. Families are as unique as people, and when they break, their fracture pattern is theirs alone.

A large-scale study published in the *Journal of Perinatal Education (JPE)* in 2012 investigated the impressions bereaved parents have on how to parent older siblings through stillbirth, and the advice they would offer to newly bereaved parents on this topic. In this study, an online questionnaire was administered to 1,200 grieving parents, although ultimately only 400 parental responses were incorporated into the study. Separate questionnaires were administered to mothers and fathers, and all families were required to already have a living child at the time of stillbirth. Ultimately, there were two key takeaway points on parenting siblings through stillbirth:
1) Make the stillborn baby and the loss real for the siblings
2) Take the siblings' resources and prerequisites into account

The overwhelming advice from bereaved parents was to help your living children understand their sibling has died, in a manner that respects your living children's unique capacity to process the resulting intense emotions. I love this advice because it both honors your living children's right to grieve, and the individuality of those children's personalities and internal emotional resources.

The *JPE* study further broke their parenting advice down into subcategories, as described below.
1) Make the stillborn baby and the loss real for the siblings
    a) Experience the stillborn baby

       i) Many of the parents who chose to participate in the study encouraged older siblings to meet their younger sibling in the hospital. We did not do this for many reasons; however, physically meeting their stillborn baby brother or sister can be helpful for siblings in understanding that they are "real." We instead opted to utilize the photography services provided by the non-profit Now I Lay Me Down to Sleep to provide our daughter with photographs of her brother without bringing her to the hospital. A companion point to the advice to bring older siblings to the hospital was to have an additional trusted adult present to help guide them. The bereaved parents in this study emphasized it was not realistic to expect bereaved parents to prepare and guide their living child through the death of their sibling immediately after learning of it themselves, and that a separate, trusted, respectful adult is helpful in filling this role while in the hospital.

  b) Get siblings involved
       i) The advice to have siblings involved refers to funeral or memorial preparations. An older sibling may want to pick a poem or song for the service, or may want to choose a stuffed animal to go into their little sibling's casket. Here again, having a separate, trusted adult with the primary responsibility of helping the older sibling is extremely beneficial, as the bereaved parents will likely be overwhelmed by the reality of their child's funeral.

  c) Inform and communicate
       i) Uniformly, advice from bereaved parents and child psychologists alike is to be forthright and

direct when it comes to telling your children their little brother or sister has died. Child psychologists recommend using clear language, such as died and death, and to avoid euphemisms such as passed away or went to sleep, as these euphemisms may make it hard for young children to understand what has happened (or may make them afraid of falling asleep!).

d) Create memories

   i) It is important to let the bereaved siblings create and collect memories, just as it is important for the bereaved parents to create and collect memories. It is for this reason that many of the bereaved parents in the study recommended older siblings come to the hospital. I would like to emphasize however, that the hospital and funeral are not the only opportunities for your living children to create memories of their sibling. Mementos of your deceased child, including photographs, clothes they wore, blankets they were wrapped in, or their tiny foot and handprints also serve as means to memorialize them. Memories can also be created years in the future as you include your child in family rituals and honor their legacy. To this day, we are constantly creating memories of Kegan, whether by performing acts of kindness in his memory, including his picture in family photos, or attending Remembrance Walks in his honor. There are myriad ways to create memories moving forward, parents need not worry that there is a defined critical period after which memories and associations can no longer be made. Memories can be created for as long as love is acted upon.

2) Take the siblings' resources and prerequisites into account
    a) Respect the siblings' feelings
        i) The parents in this study emphasized the distinction between encouraging and coercing the living children to meet with or discuss their deceased sibling. Living children should be trusted to participate on their own terms, with their own understanding of what they are or are not comfortable with doing or saying. Their grief should be taken seriously, and their point of view honored as valid. Furthermore, it should be emphasized that nothing they can say or do will be wrong or taboo, and that all thoughts or feelings, no matter how confusing or unexpected, will be honored. It is crucial to explain that the living siblings do not "have" to feel a certain way. It is also crucial to make space for the living siblings' grief, and to make it clear to them that they can express it whenever and however they desire. The living siblings have waited a long time for their baby brother or sister, and just as the bereaved parents are proud of their baby, they are also likely proud of their deceased sibling. Allow space for them to express love for and pride in their sibling, in whatever form it takes. Most importantly, respect the individuality of the living children's personality, internal emotional resources, and sensitivity. They are unique individuals, and will, or won't, express their grief in the way that suits them. And finally, crucially, never forget that

even though the stillborn baby has died, they are still the living children's sibling.
  b) Adapt to the siblings' ages
     i) Be sensitive to the age of the living children and anticipate that any mourning or leave-taking actions will be developmentally aligned with that age. Children may need to have their sibling's death explained to them multiple times, or they may oscillate between sad and happily distracted by play. Young children also frequently "play-out" their large emotions, which may result in your living children acting out the process of childbirth, your child dying, or a funeral. Try not to be alarmed or upset when you see this, it is a normal way for children to process their large emotions. Similarly, try not to be alarmed if you DON'T see them play-out their large emotions as every child's grief is unique. Children may also process their large emotions through singing, drawing, or telling stories. Try to sit with your children in whatever developmental stage they are in and be as forthright with them as you can within the bounds of their age and internal emotional resources.

After Kegan died, one of our primary worries was the effect his death was going to have on Keira. While I knew parents who had experienced stillbirth, I did not know anyone who already had an older living child at the time of their baby's death. Karol and I knew not to ask those who hadn't gone through stillbirth for advice on this, we instinctively sensed that they would urge us to downplay or deny Kegan's existence to Keira, but we didn't know who to turn to for help. We ultimately sought advice from both our grief therapist and Keira's pediatrician. Reassuringly, the advice we received from each of them was completely congruent—they urged us to discuss Kegan's death with Keira directly, to repeat the conversation as often as she requested, to make it clear that any feelings she had were welcome, to emphasize Kegan's death was nobody's fault and that no one else was in danger of dying, and lastly, to let her see us be sad.

The advice to let Keira see our sadness at losing her brother startled us at first. Weren't we supposed to be the rock for our child's emotions? Weren't we supposed to be stalwart and stoic, a place she could turn to know all was safe? Wouldn't letting her see us mourn her brother be upsetting to her? Our grief therapist explained to us that by not mourning Kegan in front of her, we would inadvertently teach her that we don't miss people after they die; we would inadvertently teach her we wouldn't miss her if she died. And, incredibly detrimentally, we would inadvertently teach her that she herself wasn't allowed to grieve, that upsetting or negative emotions must be suppressed. Of course, our therapist and Keira's pediatrician both emphasized we should be in control of the intensity of our emotions around her, that while it is helpful for our daughter to see us be sad, it is not helpful for her to see us lying on the floor sobbing…ultimately, we reserved the floor sobbing for naptimes or when she was out of the house. Ever the planner, I readily came up with an easy phrase to explain any sorrow that Keira may witness. When she saw I was sad, I would simply tell her I was missing her brother, because I love ALL my babies and miss any of them when they are away from me. Not only did this emphasize to her that it's acceptable to be sad when you are away from someone you miss, it reinforced to her that as one of my babies, I also love and miss her when we are apart.

The topic of death is foreign to many young children, and to learn about it by losing an immediate family member is excruciatingly unfair. Young children may become afraid someone else they love will die, especially their mother if she is still in the hospital. Karol and I repeatedly emphasized to Keira that even though Kegan was dead, we (and she) were safe and that we were present with her. Keira, ever the inquisitive little girl, had a multitude of questions about what death was and why Kegan in particular had died. These were heartrending questions to answer, especially in the first month when we were still waiting on our precious son's autopsy report and had no idea what caused his death. We explained that when a person dies, their body stops working and sometimes, especially when it comes to babies in their mommy's tummy, it's hard to figure out the cause, but that there always is a cause. That people don't just randomly die. This prompted the intensely painful question of what was the cause (we didn't know!), and even more painful to hear, the question of whether it was anyone's fault. Of course, here she was really asking, was it my fault? Did Kegan die because I had (perfectly normal) worries and jealousy about sharing Mommy and Daddy? We hurriedly reassured her it was no one's fault. Her asking us this question was a serendipitous insight into her worries about the kind of big sister she was and emphasized to us the importance of reinforcing what a wonderful sister she was, and always had been.

As Keira has aged, we have been introduced to another aspect of stillbirth—how she approaches her brother's death within her own social circle. From early on, we modeled answering the question of how many children we have with "one living and one deceased" and Keira has picked up on this. She doesn't readily volunteer information about her brother to strangers, but neither does she shy away from sharing about him. When friends ask about siblings, she matter-of-factly tells them she had a brother who died, before running off to play whatever game she is interested in. At this stage, she has only brought him up on her own with a few, very trusted friends or adults. She is not ashamed of his existence and will readily talk about him, but waits to open her heart up to those she deeply trusts. Karol and I have had to try to always be one step ahead of her, telling our story to her teachers and close friends' parents before she broaches the topic herself. We have taken our cues from her, and try to provide an environment that honors her individuality and emphasizes our love and gratitude for her, while also allowing space for her own unique grief. Our sweet, strong, empathetic little girl has been an inspiration to watch as she navigates the loss of her brother. She approaches his death with a wistful, matter-of-fact nature and dreams of one day becoming a "baby doctor" so "no one else's baby brother will ever have to die."

Karol and I have opted not to have a third child after losing Kegan, however many parents do go on to have additional children after experiencing stillbirth. For this reason, any discussion of siblings of stillborn infants necessarily must include the children born after stillbirth. While I cannot speak personally to the unique challenges these parents face during and after their pregnancies, I can provide a brief summary of pertinent medical literature. There has been a great deal of debate over the influence of stillbirth on subsequent pregnancies and parent-child attachment. Physicians generally recommend waiting a specified time period after stillbirth to conceive again, but that length of time varies by doctor. The World Health Organization recommends waiting two years after a live birth and six months after a miscarriage to conceive again, but they do not, at this time, offer formal recommendations on conceiving after stillbirth.

Health and psychological organizations emphasize that prior to conceiving after stillbirth, not only does the mother's body need time to heal, but both parents also need to emotionally process the death of their stillborn child. Some studies have suggested that becoming pregnant less than a year after giving birth to a stillborn child is associated with increased depression, anxiety, PTSD symptoms, and disordered attachment with the subsequent child, however other studies indicate subsequent pregnancies are associated with decreased depression and may facilitate emotional healing in the parents. As with everything in stillbirth, I suspect it has a great deal to do with the individuality of the parents in question, and where they are on their unique grief journey. Studies on attachment between the parent and subsequent child indicate the vital importance of distinguishing the two pregnancies so they do not become conflated into "one big pregnancy." A study published in 2001 from the *Journal of Child Psychology and Psychiatry* found that infants of mothers with unresolved grief (as measured through the Adult

Attachment Interview) showed higher levels of disorganized attachment than infants of mothers who resolved their prior loss. Note that to resolve a prior loss does not mean to "get over" or "forget it." It simply means you accept and integrate your child's death as part of your life story. Parents with unresolved grief are more likely to conflate subsequent pregnancies with the pregnancy that ended in stillbirth, whereas parents with resolved grief are able to separate the pregnancies and children more effectively in their minds.

Following stillbirth, parents show heightened concern over their living children. Death isn't something that happens to other people's children anymore, risk isn't something you can afford to look away from. Pregnancies after stillbirth are characterized by intense anxiety and increased medicalization; parents are more on the alert for signs of danger to their baby and make more frequent visits to their doctor or the urgent care with concerns. Parents may also be less inclined to bond with their baby during pregnancy for fear of losing them, but then show increased protectiveness of children after they are born. In my personal experience, this increased anxiety and protectiveness isn't only applicable to the children born after stillbirth. Karol and I both grew increasingly anxious about Keira after losing Kegan, obsessively worrying over the slightest sniffle or rash. In a very real way, we have lost the ability to accept the normal risks of childhood.

While childhood grief is not commonly acknowledged by society, children born both before and after stillbirth unquestionably grieve their deceased sibling. Regardless of whether children watched their mommy's tummy grow big with their little brother, or they only have pictures of the big sister they never knew, they love and miss their sibling. They mourn their brother or sister, in many cases for the rest of their life. Study after study has repeatedly emphasized three key ways to help a child who has lost a sibling through their subsequent grief.
1) Recognize and acknowledge the child's grief
2) Include both living and deceased children in family rituals
3) Keep the memory of the deceased baby alive in the family

So often after stillbirth, friends and family rally around the parents and forget any living children. If living children are remembered, it is in the context of logistics, of figuring out who will take care of them while the parents are grieving or at therapy sessions. Children are the invisible grievers, the forgotten grievers. The abandoned grievers. However, after watching Keira these past years and after talking to other parents, including parents whose children were born after their older sibling already passed, I can confidently say this—children absolutely grieve. Children love, miss, long for, and yes, sometimes get jealous of, their deceased sibling. Just because a child has died, that doesn't mean they aren't the living children's sibling anymore. The most important thing we can do for our living children in guiding them through the grief process is simply acknowledging the reality of their experience and accepting their grief exactly as it is.

Journal Prompt:

If you have living children in addition to your stillborn child, how do you make decisions on communicating with them about their deceased sibling? How would you like communications with your current or future children about their sibling to look in the future? What are ways you can incorporate your deceased child's memory into family events and rituals? Does your family find the topic of grief to be approachable, and if not, how can you empower your living children to feel comfortable expressing their emotions regarding their deceased sibling?

CHAPTER 8: ON GRIEF TRIGGERS

"You're everywhere
Except right here
And it hurts"

~Rupi Kaur

Dear Sarah,

Lyra began the school year yesterday. She is in kindergarten, a beautiful, charming age, an age of innocence and wonder, of exploration, love, and giggles. As we watched her walk through the door of her classroom, she paused briefly, turned, waved her chubby little hand just once, and then skipped away, vanishing into the room. And Sarah, I just broke inside. The other parents around me were teary-eyed too, so no one thought anything of it, but oh, I felt as if my heart had fallen out of my body. I know it is normal to cry when your child starts school. Normal to miss the life you were living with them, normal to want lazy mornings with reading and art projects back, normal to suddenly realize how quickly they are growing and to mourn that your role in their life is becoming smaller and smaller. These are all normal reactions to their first day of school. And yet...there was more.

There was the realization that Lyra's first day of school SHOULD have been my first day alone with Liam. That her beginning of school should have been the beginning of mine and Liam's special mama/son time, but that that time will never occur. There was the realization that a phase in my own life is now over, that I need to find a new way to spend my hours now that Lyra is in school full time...and that I should have had years longer to delight in the sticky, tiring, gorgeous young-toddler-at-home phase. And finally, there was the realization that this first day of school was the last first day of school I would ever get. That I would never see a chubby hand waving goodbye for the first time, that I would never have another absolute first day of school. Oh, I know we will have first days for all the other years to come, but I will never experience sending a child to school for the very first time ever again. This is all I get.

I was crying because my time with Lyra at home was over and because my time with Liam at home would never happen. I was crying because I was witnessing a milestone he would never have, and we would never get to see him experience. And I was crying because my poor sweet girl would never get to share future first days with her brother. As I stood watching older children proudly wrap their arms around their little sibling's shoulders as they posed for first day of school photos, all I could think was, she will never get that. She will forever be a big sister without a brother. My lonely only.

At school pickup that afternoon, my mind flashed forward to what Liam's first day of school should look like. As I watched my daughter pull her backpack onto her small frame, I couldn't help but see the ghost of a smaller shape next to her, proudly fidgeting with his own pack. Sarah, at that moment, my heart physically ached for the future we will never have. Lyra and I stayed after so she could play on the playground with her new friends, which of course meant I had to make small talk with the other parents. They began narrating their troubles over managing their full, busy households, and I nodded listlessly, trying desperately to distance myself from their words. One child is just so much easier, they insisted, multiple children make everything harder, more expensive, more tiring. I slowly detached myself from the conversation, strolling away on the pretense of checking my voicemail. How could I tell them I would give anything to have their worries, anything to have to stress over picking up one child from soccer while getting the other to bed on time, anything to have to referee the early morning fights and chaos before school. How could I tell them how lucky these stresses made them? But then, Sarah, I know I am lucky as well. Liam's death has made me acutely aware of how lucky every second with Lyra is, of how sweet every hug, giggle, and yes, even every tantrum, is. I breathed down the sob rising in my throat and watched her swing from the monkey bars, drinking in the sight of her light hair glistening in the sun, her sneakers dangling above the ground before she let go, landing in a puddle of laughter.

When we arrived home, Lyra dumped her things on the ground before running into the kitchen for an after-school snack. I automatically straightened her backpack against the wall and was struck by how lonely it looked. One backpack, forever companionless. In our future, there should be two. Two little backpacks, lined up by the door. Two little sets *of shoes, scuffed with playground dirt. Two lunch pails to unpack. Two worried hearts to soothe over back-to-school anxieties, two distinct, yet similar giggles, overlapping in stories from the day. Two. Yet there is and forever will be only one, and I have to wonder if the first day of school will ever not break my heart.*

I have been lying on Liam's nursery floor staring at the ceiling all day. I am alternating between sobs and numbness, between actively breaking and feeling as if there is nothing left in me to shatter. How can I live this life when normal events tear me apart so drastically? How can I face another day when I don't know what will break me?

In trepidation,
Evelyn

Dearest Evelyn,

I hear you. I hear your fear, your sadness, your regret, and your anger. I understand. There is nothing wrong with you for feeling this way. Your trauma and loss were retriggered by Lyra beginning school. It is very normal for events or objects to serve as triggers after a loss, resulting in a wave of grief that can feel just as intense as the grief we feel in the first days after losing someone we love.

Grief triggers are an expected part of grief, as are grief waves. Early on, grief is overwhelmingly present in everything we do, and then as time passes, while it doesn't go away, it does to a certain extent subside. You get used to having your grief with you. You learn to carry it. And then one day you get triggered, perhaps by a song, or a scent, or by seeing a baby, or...by a milestone such as the first day of school, and you get knocked down by a wave of emotions. Grief waves are so powerful, so painful. The scars we had carefully built over our wounded hearts are torn off, and we are left defenseless and bleeding.

There are so many things that can trigger us, reminders of what we lost, reminders of our trauma, reminders of what we will never have. To this day, seventeen years later, I still get triggered. I still get a hollow feeling in my stomach at the sight of a smiling young mother pushing a pram down the road, or shudder away from the smell of freshly cooked bacon (my primary craving during Maddie's pregnancy). I still look away from baby clothes sections in stores and try to avoid television shows and movies that focus on death. Almost two decades later, I can still be triggered.

As time has passed, I have (to a certain extent) learned what triggers me, which helps in anticipating and preparing for the resultant wave of grief. I am able to recognize triggers for what they are, and so am able to better understand the wave of emotions I am feeling. Additionally, being exposed to so many of my triggers repeatedly over the last seventeen years has helped me build up a limited tolerance to them. While I am still triggered by the sight of hugely pregnant women, seeing them no longer results in tears. I still have a sad, wistful, broken feeling in my heart when I pass them, but most of the time, I am able to continue my day.

Triggers are completely normal, and so are grief waves. I would love to hear more about what triggers you and the shape your grief waves take. Are they as intense as your early grief? How long do they last? There is no right or wrong answer to that—some grievers find their grief waves become less intense and shorter over time, some find they are just as intense twenty years in the future and never become shorter. Grief is so individualized—there is no right or wrong way to experience grief waves, all you can do is learn what is normal for YOU.

With tenderness,
Sarah

Dear Sarah,

The shape of my grief wave...what an interesting concept. I had never thought of it like that. Well, I suppose when I get triggered, the intensity of my grief feels just as strong as right after Liam died. I feel like I am back in those early days, struggling to breathe. I want to scream and cry, and run, and not move...all at the same time. I want to crawl out of my skin and into an existence where children never die. It still feels so raw, so bloody. So present.

In terms of the duration of my grief waves, I'm not sure how to answer that. I think only time will help me determine it. We are only just now beginning to experience grief in waves instead of a constant flood. Our waves are still frequent and rapid, with only days to weeks between them to catch our breath. While we are able to give Lyra a happy existence during the day, it still feels like we are constantly being triggered and surrendering to waves of mourning at night.

I am slowly beginning to identify some of my triggers. Pregnant women and babies, of course. All baby related items. It turns out little girls with their baby siblings is a huge trigger for me. Even families with a grown son and daughter can be excruciatingly painful—I almost lost it at a restaurant the other night when a family of four was seated behind us. The family had a son and daughter, both in their twenties, and they all just looked so happy to be together, so charmed, and delighted to be spending time as a foursome. I couldn't help but look twenty years into our future and see that we would never have that. We would never have a dinner out with our two grown children, sharing stories of college, their first jobs, their travels, or anything. We would never get to see Lyra tease her little brother over his first serious girlfriend or see Liam asking his sister for college advice. That door is closed to us, forever.

Another huge trigger for me is anything related to doctors. I will drive twenty minutes out of my way to avoid seeing the hospital where Liam was born, and I am actively avoiding scheduling routine exams due to anxiety around being treated by a physician...I can't even watch TV shows that take place in hospitals! I am triggered both by the physical location of being near Liam's place of birth, as well as by anything medically related.

Do you have any advice on how to avoid being triggered? I feel like I am continually being ambushed by my own shattered heart.

With love,
Evelyn

Dear Evelyn,

Do I have any advice on how to avoid being triggered? Oh my, I wish I did! With all my heart, I wish I did! My first piece of advice on triggers is to always, always talk through any grief waves with your therapist. My therapist and I did (and still do!) a lot of work around identifying triggers. It's incredibly helpful to know if you are being triggered in the moment so that you can recognize you are entering a grief wave AND it's incredibly helpful to anticipate when you will be triggered in the future so you can prepare yourself for the possibility of a grief wave. I find that I am better able to weather grief waves when I identify them as such.

I have also found that recognizing a grief wave as just that, a wave, is helpful. Waves roll in, and waves knock you down, but they also roll out again. While grief is forever, the intensity of severe grief waves is NOT forever. Severe grief will come and go, in and out, just like ocean waves.

Lastly, I have realized I can survive waves. I have survived seventeen years of severe grief waves. When I get knocked down by a particularly strong wave, I can look at my past and say, I know I can survive this. I have survived grief waves before, and I will get through this one too. I will never stop missing Maddie, I will never stop grieving her, AND I can also know more light-hearted days are still ahead of me. I can bring her memory through the waves, through the storm, and into the sun.

With love,
Sarah

In the early days of loss, there is no respite from the suffocating flood of your grief. It overwhelms your senses, pervading every aspect of your life. It doesn't even make sense to talk about waves of grief early on, because that would imply a break from the deluge, a brief moment when you could catch your breath. You are constantly submerged, drowning in your own sadness, trauma, and loss.

As time passes, the flood slowly recedes. Some days, you find you can smile. One day, you surprise yourself with a laugh, the sound echoing both familiar and alien in your ears. As time passes, you slowly begin to figure out how to live this new existence, how to function in a world where grief is continually present, but cannot be perpetually paramount. You don't get over, you adapt.

And then one day you see a two-year-old little girl smiling at her infant brother and your heart shatters. Or you see a pregnant woman absent-mindedly stroking her swollen belly and find yourself unable to breathe. Or you see a toddler being allowed to play unsupervised by the street and are immediately blinded by both fear and a red-hot rage. You are suddenly immersed in a wave of emotions, unable to continue the conversation you were just having, unable to even see straight...ambushed by your own traitorous, broken heart.

Where do they come from, these waves? How can we go from semi-normal functioning to shattered in a second? And what can we do to protect ourselves in the future?

Grief triggers refer to anything that causes painful feelings related to your loss to resurface. These can encompass food, songs, clothes, smells, events, times of year, and even relationships. To a bereaved, traumatized parent, a trigger can be literally anything, even something that seems completely innocuous to the casual observer. One of my own personal triggers that seems completely benign to others is almond croissants. The last thing I ate before I found out Kegan had died was an almond croissant. I had gotten to the hospital early and happily crammed a warm croissant into my mouth as I cheerfully strolled the hallway to my OB's office. I have no idea if Kegan was alive or dead at that moment, but the idea that I was enjoying a pastry after he may have already died, or worse, was *dying,* makes my stomach turn. I haven't been able to look at an almond croissant since.

Some triggers are more obvious, more painfully generalizable to women who have endured stillbirth. Pregnancy triggers me, as do newborn babies. I rapidly unfollow anyone in my social media newsfeed as soon as they announce either a pregnancy or the birth of a child. This isn't because I wish them anything other than the best, it's simply because being a spectator to the yearned for reality that I came within a breath of living is too painful to bear.

Like many mothers who have endured stillbirth, I am triggered by most baby related items or events. Baby clothes, baby shoes, baby showers...if it's affiliated with babies, I can be triggered by it. The truth of the matter though, is that while my triggers encompass the entire baby stage, they are sadly not limited to it. The list of things that can trigger me is long and wide. I can be triggered by child pairings that are the age my children should be now, especially if there is an older sister and a younger brother. I can be triggered by planning annual family photos, or the first day of school. Anything related to death, funerals, and burials sends me into a downward spiral. Certain songs result in teary eyes, and the smell of baby detergent is torture.

So why do we have triggers? The scientist in me yearns to provide an answer, a logical reason, for my mind to continually ambush my heart. The answer to this question is still being debated, however, I speculate there is an evolutionary advantage to being able to be triggered, to recognizing a source of recurrent pain. Evolutionarily, recognition of recurrent dangerous stimuli would increase an animal's likelihood of survival, and thereby increase their likelihood of procreation. Recognition of dangerous stimuli would keep you alive. The smell of organic baby detergent isn't a dangerous stimulus though, so why is my body still having a reflexive response? In a very real way, my body isn't able to recognize what is and isn't dangerous in the moment, it only recognizes what stimulates a memory of extreme pain.

There are a multitude of theories as to why triggers exist. The previously described theory is a popular one, as is the theory that your painful memories become temporally "misfiled" during a traumatic event. In times of trauma or danger, your body enters "fight or flight" mode, in which a flood of hormones primes your body to either fight for survival or flee for your life. During this time, nonessential bodily functions (such as digestion) are either temporarily halted or significantly slowed. One of these functions is theorized to be the formation of short-term memories. It is theorized that memories encoded during this time are (mis)filed as "present" as opposed to "past," so when the memory is accessed later, your body responds as if the threat or trauma is still present.

Another theory is that one of the reasons triggers are so powerful is because they frequently involve the senses. The more sensory information is encoded in a memory, the more easily it is later accessed or recalled, and importantly, the more salient the memory can seem. When you encounter a triggering sensory stimulus, even in a completely innocuous context, it can consequently result in an especially intense emotional recall of the trauma or loss.

The described theories are just a few explanations of why triggers exist, and while they provide some answers, they seem to raise more questions than anything. For example, if you are having an automatic emotional reaction to a sensory stimulus, are you aware, in that moment, that you are being triggered? I think the answer to this would be, not always. Some triggers may send you back to a place of flashbacks, in which case you would (at some later point) very certainly be aware that something had triggered you. Some, however, may simply make you feel sad, or short-tempered, or just "off." It is for this reason that it is so important to discover what triggers you, so that when you encounter that trigger in the world, you can identify it as such and brace yourself for the emotional fallout within yourself that may occur.

It is essential to educate medical professionals and therapists on grief triggers so they can better help patients identify and weather them. However, the literature is largely devoid of studies investigating grief triggers. A 2021 review of medical literature from the preceding twenty years that explicitly investigated grief triggers identified only six peer-reviewed studies on the topic. Six studies, over twenty years. How can we expect patients, therapists, and medical professionals to understand and weather grief triggers if they aren't provided the opportunity to be educated on them? While it's not clear why there is such a dearth of literature on this topic, one theory is that many researchers may not understand the prevalence of grief triggers in severe grief until they themselves have experienced it. Statistically speaking, more adults experience intense, severe grief in the later decades of their life (following the death of a spouse or sibling), so it may simply be a case of first-hand experience of severe grief and the triggers associated with it more frequently occurring after researchers are either already well-established in a field or have left research entirely. While nearly everyone will have experienced some level of grief by the time they are an adult, the severe, intense grief that comes from losing an intimate relationship that was part of your everyday life statistically tends to be experienced later in life.

It is also imperative that medical professionals are made aware of common triggers in order to avoid needlessly re-traumatizing their patients. As previously described, common triggers among women who have endured stillbirth are pregnancy, seeing/visiting the hospital they gave birth in, newborns, anything baby related, and anything related to autopsies, funerals, or death. These possess a very high likelihood of triggering an intense grief wave, yet some providers are not aware these topics need to be approached with special care, or of how to increase flexibility around them. An example of how common triggers can be treated with flexibility is the postpartum appointment. Women who have endured stillbirth are postpartum, and so, still need to attend postpartum appointments. However, postpartum appointments are frequently either in the hospital they gave birth in or in the practice that managed their pregnancy, both of which are locations that are likely to be triggering. Moreover, these appointments virtually guarantee the bereaved mother will have contact with pregnant women, another very strong trigger. Bereaved mothers should not, ever, have to sit in a waiting room with expectant mothers. They should not be expected to return to the waiting room they so often frequented throughout their pregnancy, they should not be forced to be an unwilling spectator to someone else's joyful journey. Here is a place where the physician can recognize common grief triggers ahead of time and make alternate plans to accommodate the bereaved mother. For example, our OB practice's office was in the same hospital I gave birth to Kegan in, and so my postpartum appointments were already in a very triggering location. While my physician couldn't do anything about where her office was physically located, she did have me call the receptionist when I arrived to avoid me being forced to enter the waiting room. I was subsequently escorted through a backdoor to an examination room I had never been in. While this was undoubtedly more logistically challenging for everyone involved, it was absolutely the kinder, more compassionate choice.

Grief is a highly personal, individualized process, with both many commonalities and many distinctions between grievers. No one travels identical paths through grief, even those who have experienced similar losses, or even the loss of the same person. My husband and I both lost the exact same child, yet our grief experiences, although similar, are not interchangeable. We both have grief triggers, we both experience recurrent waves of grief, but these triggers and waves are not identical. While we share certain triggers (anniversaries, holidays, baby boys with a head full of dark curls), a large number of our triggers are unique to our singular personalities and experiences. Similarly, while many bereaved mothers may identify with some of the same triggers, there will be a multitude of triggers unique to each griever. It is for this reason that it is so imperative for therapists to work with each individual to identify their specific triggers and to help them develop a plan for when they are confronted by those triggers.

The importance of grief triggers needs to be emphasized among both medical professionals and grieving patients, especially given the role triggers play in the grief trajectory. Society has largely taken to issuing trigger warnings to help those who have been traumatized avoid being retriggered, but what if we were able to go one step further and use triggers to help the patient reintegrate more fully into society? What if a patient and their therapist were able to identify innocuous, everyday triggers and then, in a safe, supportive environment, do intense therapy around those triggers? If triggers are identified and discussed, we take (at least some of) their power over us away. While we may still be triggered, we will also have the knowledge that we *are* being triggered, and most importantly, *that we have survived triggers and grief waves in the past and can survive them again.*

In a very real way, we can grow our own resilience by simply seeing a grief wave for what it is. By merely identifying a grief wave as a "wave," we allow ourselves to see that it is transient. We are not immersed in an eternal flood; we are being knocked over by a wave. A wave similar to waves we have struggled through before. A wave we know we will be able to survive because our own personal history tells us we can find our feet after being knocked over. A wave we know we will overcome because our own personal history tells us that we are resilient.

The knowledge that you can survive a grief wave is, sadly, something that you can only truly acquire after experiencing multiple grief waves. The key to developing faith in your own resilience is identifying grief waves and triggers for what they are. For the griever, it is scary, confusing, and frankly, overwhelming to be plunged into grief waves in a seemingly stochastic manner. If, however, the triggers of those waves can be identified and the waves themselves precipitated, the griever can better brace themselves for the storm of emotions that will follow. By labeling grief triggers and waves, the griever increases their own resilience. The simple act of understanding what is happening within your own brain and body, *and observing the reality that you have survived waves in the past*, gives the griever a tool to weather future waves.

The data on duration and severity of grief waves over time is varied. Some data indicate that as time since the initial loss passes, grief waves become shorter in duration and less intense. Other data indicate that grief waves may become shorter in duration, but that they maintain their initial intensity. And yet more data indicate that the shape of grief waves, as measured by duration and intensity, does not change at all. Like everything with grief, grief waves are highly individualized. Most of the data does, however, agree on one aspect of grief waves, which is that they become less frequent over time. While the shape of grief waves in the years after a loss may (or may not) resemble the shape of grief waves in early grief, the waves themselves slowly begin to be more spread out. The griever is able to catch their breath. They are slowly able to reintegrate themselves into society and experience the normal joys of living. They recognize that while grief itself is immortal, individual grief waves are transient. They develop faith in their own ability to survive.

Society tells us our goal is to get through grief, to break through the dark clouds of heartbreak to the sunshine on the other side. That if we can consistently do this, we are grieving correctly, and if we cannot, there is something wrong with us, or our grief. Society tells us this, but most people who have experienced severe, intense grief know otherwise. Grief is forever. Some days your heart will be filled with sunshine, some days it will bend under the storm clouds of heartache. Some days the ocean of your heart will be smooth, some days you will drown in waves. This is normal. Grief waves are normal. As a society, we need to stop pathologizing grief triggers and grief waves. Triggers are an expected protective response after undergoing severe loss and trauma. Grief waves are an expected response when confronted with a trigger. We should instead seek to identify and understand our triggers so we can better anticipate grief waves. We should seek to recognize our grief waves so we can help ourselves through them. And medical professionals should be better equipped to both acknowledge and counsel patients about grief triggers and grief waves. The grief trajectory is not a linear road—grief manifests in constantly changing ways, so let's stop pretending experiencing it will be anything other than dynamic.

Journal Prompt:

Think back on your own grief triggers. Are they items, foods, scents, experiences, relationships? As time has passed, are you able to anticipate some of these triggers? What does the resulting grief wave look like? Does anticipating a grief wave alter the severity of that grief wave? How have your grief waves and triggers altered over time?

CHAPTER 9: ON HOLIDAYS AND ANNIVERSARIES

"Baby, all I want for Christmas is you."

~Mariah Carey

Dear Evelyn,

As the seasons turn and the days begin to grow shorter, it strikes me that this will be your first holiday season since burying Liam. I was caught completely unawares my first holiday season after losing Maddie. While I knew the holidays would be triggering, I had no idea how pervasive those triggers would be. Navigating the holidays felt like tiptoeing across a minefield—one wrong step and the fragile facade I had built around myself would implode. Truthfully, I had many implosions that first holiday season and continue to have them to this day. The holidays are hard when you have lost anyone, but especially so when you have lost a child.

It can feel as if the holidays are a constant barrage of taunts, a neverending volley of reminders of all that you have lost. Beginning in the fall, you are inundated with images of smiling families at pumpkin patches, which transition into statements of how "blessed" or "grateful" everyone is at Thanksgiving, and as the seasons turn again, holiday cards full of intact families begin to ambush you daily via the post. Pictures of sweet little ones sitting on Santa's lap or wholesome images of complete families at the Christmas tree farm are a constant reminder of the holiday cheer your family SHOULD be partaking in. Finally, Christmas morning rolls around, and with it, photographs of chubby-cheeked toddlers in rumpled candy-cane pajamas holding stockings stuffed far too full of toys and chocolates. I found the pain to be unbearable. It was actually due to the pain of the first holiday season that Paul and I implemented a "rule" for ourselves that I would like to share. We avoid all forms of social media on holidays. Whether it be Thanksgiving, the Fourth of July, St. Patrick's Day, or Christmas, if there is an occasion with an increased likelihood of us being forced to bear witness to the wholeness of other families, we avoid social media and instead focus on our own insular family unit.

I wanted to reach out and offer extra support as we approach the holiday season. Remember, any feeling you have during this time is "right." You do not have to express a cheer you do not feel, and similarly, if you do find yourself enjoying moments or even days of the holidays, that is also perfectly fine. In the early days of grief, I struggled with extreme guilt after joyful feelings. I would berate myself for enjoying even the briefest moment of festivities, as if by doing so I was betraying Maddie. I wasn't betraying her—I was being human. And humans ricochet between emotions. We can go from heartbroken to giggles in minutes, and that doesn't make any of those emotions any less valid or true. Any emotions or feelings you have are exactly right, for you, in that particular moment. There is no such thing as a "wrong" feeling or emotion; emotions can't be wrong, they simply are.

With love,
Sarah

Dearest Sarah,

Thank you, as always, for your insight into the world of grief. You are right, I have been feeling lower recently. There has been a deep feeling of dread creeping into my days as those days have shortened and grown colder. Everywhere I look, I am assaulted with images of intact families enjoying the season, complete families that are blissfully unaware of how extremely fortunate they are.

Additionally, Liam's death and birth occurred in February, in the lull between the holidays and Valentine's Day. As the holidays approach, I can almost hear a steady beat marching us closer and closer to his birthday, to the day our hearts shattered. As the nights get colder and the leaves change, I am reminded of how joyful I felt this time last year and have to wonder if I will ever feel pure joy and happiness again. I remember going to pumpkin patches last fall and Lyra picking out Liam's "first" pumpkin, I remember squealing relatives rubbing my swollen belly at Thanksgiving as they tried to guess what we would name our son, and I remember Lyra gleefully sitting on Santa's lap and telling him he would be bringing presents for TWO kiddos the following year. She was wrong, of course. Liam died seven weeks later. Last year, this season held so much delight and anticipation. Now it brings only dread. I would say I wish I could fast forward through the holidays, but that would bring me directly to Liam's anniversaries, and I can't even begin to comprehend how I will survive them.

During these days, these heartbreaking days so full of joy for everyone else, I also feel the need to remind the world my son existed. The world wants to forget him, they want to forget his loss and our subsequent sadness. And so, I feel the need to remind them of him, to remind them that our little boy should be here. Yet at the same time, I feel guilty for bringing sadness into their seasonal joy. As if by being true to my son and myself, I have ruined their holiday. Furthermore, I sometimes will even find myself enjoying parts of the holidays, and am then instantly plunged into another deep well of guilt. I am conflicted on a daily basis, snapping between the emotional extremes of the season. During festivities especially, I feel so bitter at the loss of my son, but am simultaneously so grateful for the presence of my daughter. While I adore the life we have with Lyra, I also wish so many parts of it were different. I am confronted with a cacophony of conflicting emotions, ricocheting from one sentiment to the next.

I have tried to live my life with a focus on positive emotions, but truthfully, it just is not possible currently. I am overwhelmed with feelings of longing, guilt, loneliness, anger, and extreme envy. Why do other parents get to carve pumpkins with all of their children? Why do other parents get to list every one of their children's names as what they are grateful for at the Thanksgiving table? Why do other families get Christmas mornings full of squabbling kids and laughter? What did we do wrong? Why was this taken from us? I know focusing on what others have is a recipe for unhappiness, but it is so hard not to when you are confronted with pictures of intact families at every turn. The holiday season...it is just impossible. And yet, I know the season after, the season of Liam's death and birth, will be even more excruciating. I am exhausted. I am completely spent and can't imagine how I will have the fortitude to survive the coming months.

In weariness,
Evelyn

Dearest Evelyn,

I wish I could reach through these letters and wrap you in a hug. You will survive the coming months. You will. You will because you have already survived so much. And sweet Evelyn, I know you can survive this on your own, but also know you do not have to. You have David, and you have me.

I so clearly hear the pain and anxiety you are expressing, both about the holidays and Liam's anniversaries. After many years of stumbling through the holidays, I have finally come up with some strategies I would love to share with you.

The first is the knowledge that you do not have to participate in any holiday activity that makes you uncomfortable or heightens your sadness. There is an incredible amount of pressure put on the bereaved to return to "normal" holiday joy, but society forgets our worlds will never be "normal" again. Rest assured in the knowledge that you are under no obligation to partake in any dinner, party, or event that will cause you increased pain. With that being said, it is helpful to inform those around you of your decision. I have found that friends and family are far more understanding of my decisions to pass on certain holiday functions if I communicate those decisions to them. You certainly don't have to describe in detail why you are passing on attending a function (as the saying goes, "'No' is a full sentence"), but if you feel supported describing the emotions around your decision, it may be helpful in order to prevent future conflict or to manage future expectations. Paul and I find it is also helpful to check in with each other and our living children regarding holiday events. We all have different ways of mourning Maddie and so all have different needs in terms of how to incorporate her into the holidays. One of the ways we have been able to best navigate the holidays is by making sure everyone in our immediate family unit feels comfortable expressing their holiday desires around Maddie, and importantly, that we are open to hearing each other's needs.

The second strategy for navigating hard days is to make a plan ahead of time. Paul and I sit down every year with our son and living daughter and together discuss what we want the holidays and Maddie's anniversaries to look like, how we want Maddie included and celebrated, and who we want to interface with on the days in question. We have also built traditions around her that make it easy for our extended families to include her in the holidays, and have further established traditions within our own internal family unit in terms of how we will honor her. We know the overall structure for how we will spend her anniversaries, but also leave room for last minute changes and flexibility. It is hugely healing to include Maddie in our family traditions, and, by having traditions and discussing anticipated plans ahead of time, we take a great deal of the uncertainty and anxiety out of triggering days.

Lastly, I would love to share a new technique I only recently learned myself in terms of holding space for the many conflicting emotions holidays and anniversaries bring. There is a semantic technique in grief literature of replacing the word "but" in our emotional descriptors with the word "and." The tenet is that conflicting emotions can be present within your soul simultaneously, and that that is not only acceptable, but is completely normal. By replacing "but" with "and," you allow yourself the grace to feel the beauty of your love and heartbreak without judgment, exactly as they exist. This technique is helpful every day of the year, but especially on holidays and anniversaries. I am grateful for the children I have AND I miss my daughter. I am filled with joy watching my husband in the role of father AND I wish I could stitch up the pieces of his shattered heart. I am happy for my friends with complete families AND I live in constant fear of something happening to their children AND I wish my life had played out the same way. I am grateful AND I miss. I am filled with love AND I am filled with longing. I am joyful AND I am heartbroken. I think one of the biggest things I have learned the last few years is the "buts" don't help the hurting among us, on any day, but especially on the hard, triggering days. Allowing for the ambiguity of "and" allows us to see ourselves and each other as we really are. Joyful, devastated, strong, heartbroken, fearful, and brave. We are all of these, every day. So, this anniversary, this holiday season, this particular painful, beautiful day, I will be beyond grateful for my husband, son, and living daughter, AND I will miss my first born.

With love,
Sarah

I have a complicated relationship with holidays. I love them; I adore the decorations, the food, the traditions, the excited, cozy feeling of celebrating with your most loved and treasured people and yet...they break my heart. They highlight Kegan's absence in our memories and futures, shining a spotlight on the gaping hole in our family.

Non-grievers tend to think only the large, traditional family holidays are triggering for the grieving, and furthermore, that this exacerbated pain diminishes after the first holiday season. Both of these assumptions are wrong on multiple fronts. While large family holidays (*e.g.*, Mother's Day, Father's Day, Thanksgiving, Christmas) are excruciating, my pain is not limited to these holidays. All holidays shatter me, as all holidays shatter many of the grieving. Halloween—the last holiday I had with Kegan. New Year's—forever bringing me further in time from him. Valentine's Day—the holiday for those you love, the holiday for which I already had his adorable little man outfit, complete with suspenders and a "tie" sewn onto his onesie, hanging neatly in his closet. Even St. Patrick's Day—the first holiday I celebrated after becoming pregnant with him, the first holiday belly photo I took. The hardest holidays without a doubt are the bigger ones, but truthfully, all holidays are hard, and continue to be, years after his death.

Parents who have buried a baby often speak of wanting to skip the holidays, of wanting to fast forward from October through January and to hopscotch over the remaining holidays scattered throughout the year. They speak of the impossible pain of seeing full family units posed around a turkey, and of the suffering Christmas cards littered with images of babies brings. They describe the heartbreak resulting from social media posts on Valentine's Day, as they scroll through image after image of everyone else's heart-clad "Little Loves" holding up homemade shoebox mailboxes. And they recoil from the all-encompassing agony of Mother's Day and Father's Day, of holidays dedicated to celebrating parenthood when their own parenthood has been so cruelly ripped away from them. This avoidance of, even repulsion from, holidays is incredibly common amongst all grievers, but I think must be especially pronounced for bereaved parents. I had no idea how painful a loving, cheerful holiday could be until I myself longed to share love and holiday cheer with a little one who wasn't here to receive them.

While I now shy away from all holidays, my personal least favorite holiday since Kegan's death is Thanksgiving. Kegan was due the week before Thanksgiving and was born on November 7th. We had joked about him being our tiny turkey, our little butterball of the holidays. My struggle with Thanksgiving is therefore due both to its temporal proximity to my son's death and birth, and also to the nature of the holiday itself. Thanksgiving is about giving thanks, about being grateful for what we have, instead of focusing on what we don't, so where does that leave you when you've been so hugely cheated by death? Are you irreparably broken if your sadness and longing are so great that they cannot be overcome even for a day, if, despite your best efforts at frivolity, you can't manage to wallpaper over the gaping hole in your heart for twenty-four hours? Despite what society may tell you, the answer to that question is no. You aren't broken, you aren't faulty. You are human, with intricate, multifaceted emotions. The central tenet of Thanksgiving, being grateful for what we have, is a beautiful sentiment, but being told it is faulty to also miss that which is lacking is far too simple and doesn't allow for the complexity of humanity. Since Kegan has died, I have learned how vital it is to hold space for each other's losses as well as our joys, to not mask the intricate reality of our lives but to hold space for sadness and longing and truth. It turns out, humans are incredibly complicated, and our emotions are far more complex than the simplicity of "enjoy the holidays" allows.

I have further discovered that while there is a great deal of comfort offered the first holiday season, that support largely evaporates by the time the second holiday season rolls around. By the time the second holiday season rears its highly decorated face, we are expected to have a better handle on our emotions. We are expected to have come to terms with our loss, and to not remind the festive partygoers around us that holidays aren't happy for everyone. We are expected to keep quiet, have an eggnog, and not cast a pall over anyone else's celebrations. There is literature, however, that backs up what any grieving parent will tell you—their heart has not mended itself by the time their second Thanksgiving rolls around. In fact, many grieving parents report the second year as being harder than the first, due to both rescinded social support and to the shock of their child's death abating. During year one, painful as it is, we are partially protected by shock. By the time year two rolls around, that shock has (largely) been replaced by cold, hard reality.

Grief and counseling literature offer a myriad of tools and suggestions to grievers on how to survive the holidays. Psychologists and therapists report there are simple steps the bereaved can take to make the holidays a little more palatable, a little less triggering, and perhaps slightly easier to bear. This field of literature describes the strategy of the "3 Cs" to approach holidays after loss: Choose, Communicate, and Compromise. The bereaved can Choose what they would like to do, Communicate these needs to anyone affected, and Compromise if these needs are at odds with other intimately bereaved family members.

What does it mean to Choose? As a bereaved parent, you may not want to participate in many of the available holiday activities. Holidays center around family, children, and togetherness, and any or all of those may be triggering. We are often under the false assumption that we are required to participate in all available holiday activities, but the reality is we can Choose what we feel comfortable partaking in. You don't have to participate in every activity you are invited to, or even those that you traditionally partook in before your child died. You can assess an activity, decide if you think it will trigger or soothe you, and Choose if you would like to attend. Notably, you can also Choose to change your mind regarding that activity. If, after arriving at an event, you realize it is too triggering, you can Choose to leave. These are your rights as any person, but especially as a bereaved person. No one has the right to pressure you to be anywhere that you don't want to be or that is harmful to your mental health.

What does it mean to Communicate? It is vital to Communicate your choices about what you will and won't participate in. By managing others' expectations, you can preempt pressure and hurtful comments about not participating in certain events. If your decision affects others, you can simply inform them of your choice ahead of time, and, if you want to, may also divulge why you made that decision. You are under no obligation to describe why an event is too much or may be triggering, however, if you feel able to, it may help your loved ones support you better or be more sensitive to your needs in the future. It is also essential to check in and Communicate with other affected grievers. All grief is unique and individual grievers may have different needs and comfort levels during the holidays. What is acceptable to my husband may be highly triggering to me, and an activity we both may be tempted to skip may be incredibly meaningful to our daughter. For this reason, it is helpful for bereaved parents and siblings to Communicate their individual needs and desires, and, importantly, *for them to be receptive to hearing those desires from each other.*

What does it mean to Compromise? Individual needs and desires from grievers during a holiday celebration will almost certainly vary. As such, Compromises will have to be made. I strongly believe that the grief needs of the most intimately associated family members (the parents and siblings) trump any desire from extended family to have a "normal" holiday, but within even the intimate family circle, there will likely be discord around what are and are not triggering activities. For this reason, individual grievers should listen to each other's needs, and assess how they can best support each other while also honoring their own realities. This is especially pertinent to families with living children. The first year after Kegan died, I wanted to completely skip Thanksgiving and Christmas. I had no desire to celebrate family holidays while awaiting an autopsy report. However, we had a two-year-old daughter, so skipping the holidays simply wasn't an option. We could not, in good faith, ask her to forgo the holidays; it would have served our purposes, but would have been incredibly unfair to her. Instead, we Compromised. We looked for ways to honor my desire to avoid the triggers of the holidays, while still providing her with joy and stability. In place of a large family Thanksgiving gathering, we took our immediate family on a trip to Canada. We honored my need to avoid stating what I was grateful for around a table full of smiling extended relatives, and also honored Keira's desire to do a special activity with her parents. For the Christmas season, we tried to similarly Compromise; we incorporated Kegan into the holiday by donating and helping others in his name, and on Christmas Day, focused inward on our immediate family members, avoiding falsely jovial phone calls with extended relatives. We gave our daughter the best Christmas we were able to, but did not stretch ourselves to put a facade of happiness on for our adult relatives. We prioritized and honored all immediately affected family members' needs and realities.

As time has passed, we have felt a subtle pushing back at our desire to include Kegan in our day-to-day lives, including the holidays. For this reason, it has been incredibly helpful to us to establish new holiday traditions that explicitly include him. Kegan's memory is easily incorporated into our holidays because we have specifically built traditions around him. For example, like many families, we have a visual representation of counting down the days to Christmas. Some families use a traditional calendar, whereas others, like us, use a chain of linked papers representing the days until Christmas, with expectant children gleefully ripping one link off the chain each day. We have modified our Christmas countdown chain slightly to include our son; we write acts of kindness on each link in memory of Kegan and so each day, perform an act of kindness or charity in his memory. We create this chain every Thanksgiving as a family, with Keira taking an active role in deciding how we will commemorate her little brother in the coming days. In this way, our family actively, exuberantly celebrates Kegan on a daily basis in the lead up to Christmas. We further include Kegan in our Christmas decorations—his personalized stocking sits folded on the mantle, and we add an ornament to the tree in his memory every year. While our holiday celebrations do center around providing Keira with joyful experiences, we provide easy, visual means to celebrate and include Kegan in our festivities as well.

There are many methods whereby families can incorporate their deceased child into holiday traditions throughout the year. They may opt to visit their baby's grave on Mother's Day, decorate the table with their birth flower on Valentine's Day, perform acts of charity in their name on New Year's, or perhaps light a sparkler for them on July 4th. The important thing is to establish what new ritual works for your family, and to allow flexibility and grace if that tradition evolves. Our family hikes and blows bubbles to Kegan on Mother's Day and Father's Day. This hiking tradition is dual purpose—hiking itself has a healing, calming effect, but perhaps even more crucial to us on those days, disappearing into nature allows us to avoid locations crowded with intact families. Similarly, blowing bubbles to Kegan is dual purpose—it is a way for us to visually communicate with our son, but even more vital, is a way for Keira to celebrate her brother in a child's language of joy and play.

Anniversaries related to a stillborn child's death and birth are indescribably painful; for me, Kegan's death and birth anniversaries are more painful than any of the holidays. Not only are death and birth anniversaries a trigger for the grief and trauma of losing your child, they are a cruel reminder of the birthday celebration you should be planning, the milestones your baby should have achieved, and every milestone and celebration they will miss in the future. Many grieving parents are further triggered by the season of their child's death, and the traditional events that occur within that season. For our family, fall has come to symbolize our son's loss, a visualization of life turning to death, of the emptiness that replaces vitality.

As Kegan's anniversaries approached that first year, I was in a constant state of panic. How could we mark his birthday? I certainly didn't feel as if we could celebrate it, but I also wanted to honor his memory, to ensure the world wouldn't forget him. After multiple days of panic, Karol and I finally sat down and discussed what we each wanted his birthday to mean or include and, together, made a plan for the day. This planning discussion was key as it took an element of uncertainty, and thus at least some anxiety, out of his birthday. By making a plan for how to spend

Kegan's death and birth days ahead of time, we were able to claim a little more power over those days, and so felt a little less helpless and panicked as they approached. We ultimately decided we wanted his anniversaries to be a time for spreading good in the world, for his death and birth days to not only be days of sadness, but to also be days of kindness and charity. We asked our friends and family to join us in performing acts of kindness on those days in a movement Karol dubbed "Kegan's Kindness," and created Kegan's Kindness cards explaining his story and legacy for distribution. In this way, Kegan's anniversaries became days for good, and our heartbreak, while not any less, was channeled into love for the world.

As the years have passed, we have collected and treasured stories of good being done in our son's name from around the globe; one woman in Sweden performs forest cleanups with her toddlers, another woman in Washington D.C. annually takes her elementary-aged children to sort food at a homeless shelter in early November…the stories pour in every fall, bringing comfort to our broken hearts. Every year on Kegan's birthday, our own family unit donates requested items to a local women and children's shelter in Kegan's name before disappearing into the mountains for a peaceful hike. We pick up trash along the trail, and consciously watch for opportunities to show others goodness or kindness throughout the day. Our hearts are still completely shattered on these days, but by having a plan, we can approach them without panic. By creating a tradition and legacy for our boy, we can approach his anniversaries with a sense of purpose and pride for the difference his life has made in the world.

For many parents, the days leading up to the anniversary may be harder than the anniversary itself. The dread of an impending date compounds with grief, completely overwhelming the bereaved parent. It is helpful to recognize this and give yourself grace in the days (weeks) leading up to your child's anniversary. I try to schedule extra time to exercise in the weeks leading up to Kegan's death, and actively avoid making important decisions during this time. I also recognize I will not be the parent and partner I strive to be during those days; I will likely be more short-tempered and less joyful. By giving myself grace to experience those emotions, not only do I not berate myself when I struggle, but I actually am better able to recognize those struggles and self-regulate. I am better able to recognize when I am being impatient or irascible, take a deep breath, and then realign with my husband or daughter. Similarly, as previously described, I find it extremely helpful to make a plan during the days preceding Kegan's anniversaries for how we will spend the anniversaries themselves. So often in grief, we feel powerless and small, but by simply making a plan, we can assert power over an incredibly painful day. Notably, it is imperative to communicate this plan in advance to those affected by it, and to compromise with them to ensure everyone's needs are met. As an example of meeting everyone's individual grief needs, our birthday plans for Kegan always specifically include blowing bubbles, as Keira has indicated this is a meaningful way for her to commemorate her brother. We also discuss ahead of time who we do and don't want to communicate with on both anniversaries and holidays. By anticipating and establishing expectations within our family unit, we are better able to honor every individual's grief and needs.

The pressure to host a perfect holiday gathering or birthday party is massive during the best of conditions. Even with a fully intact family, supportive relatives, and cheer in your heart, planning these occasions can be stressful. How much more taxing are they then when combined with the death of your child, society's denial of your pain, and deep, unabiding longing and sadness? It is imperative to give ourselves grace around holidays and anniversaries, to recognize that we will not be the best version of ourselves on those days and that, despite all efforts, the days will not be the best versions of themselves. After Kegan died, I wanted holidays and anniversaries to incorporate his memory perfectly, as if by flawlessly memorializing him, I could somehow make partial amends for losing him. I was putting intense, unbearable pressure on myself, and inadvertently making already challenging days even harder to bear. As time has passed, I have learned strategies to approach these days, and have also learned the vital importance of granting grace to myself and other grievers on triggering days. I have embraced the strategy of the "3 Cs" and now strive to Choose holiday activities that soothe my heart, Communicate my plans to those affected by them, and Compromise with the needs of other bereaved family members. I have learned to make anticipatory plans for how to spend triggering days, and so take away the added anxiety of uncertainty on those days. Perhaps most importantly, I have learned to have flexibility and to give additional grace during emotionally tumultuous dates.

Holidays and anniversaries will always hurt for the simple reason that Kegan will never be present for them. He will never experience Christmas, he will never experience Valentine's Day, or July 4th. He will never blow birthday candles out, and we will never have the joy of picking out his birthday presents. These days will always be painful. There are ways to make them easier to bear, however. Including Kegan in holiday traditions is hugely healing for our family and has the added benefit of helping extended relatives know how we want them to commemorate him. Bereaved parents need their child to be remembered on holidays and have every right to expect friends and family to respect that wish. Making plans for how to spend triggering days in advance is also hugely helpful, provided these plans allow for adaptability on the day in question. Lastly, giving grace to yourself and other grievers empowers the bereaved to feel the fullness of their emotions. The holidays will never be what we want, but there is room in them for loss, heartbreak, joy, and laughter. When it comes down to it, holidays and anniversaries are really just a celebration of love. And love, I have found, is the one place you can always find your baby.

Journal Prompt:

How would you like to see your son or daughter commemorated during the holidays? What are some traditions you can establish around them, and who would you like to include in these traditions? Are there physical keepsakes that memorialize them which you can also incorporate into your holidays? Similarly, how would you like to honor your child's legacy on their birthday? What would be healing for you and your immediate family? Are there places you can visit where you feel closer to your child? Who would you like to interact with on this day, and in what capacity?

CHAPTER 10: ON GRIEF OVER TIME

"There is life after death because love never dies. I wanted my son to make a difference in the world. And even though he never drew a breath, he did. I am his mother. I carried him once. I carry him still. Even death cannot take that away. I will be his life after death."

~Kristen Wood (bereaved mother, *Still Standing* magazine)

Dear Sarah,

Is it true that grief lessens with time? I was speaking to my mother the other day and she told me, "I promise, you won't always feel this way," and honestly, it left me so confused. On the one hand, it enraged me to hear my grief belittled. How does she know I won't always feel this way? Unless I have another sibling she's never mentioned, then she's speaking from a place of zero relevant experience. Oh, I know she's experienced other losses in her life, but nothing like this, nothing so shattering and final as burying your son. Truthfully, I found it to be a very dismissive statement. Even if I won't always feel this way in the future, that statement certainly doesn't help me in the present! But then, I began to wonder...is she right? Will this pain subside with time? And, moreover, do I want it to?

The thought of my pain over Liam lessening is honestly terrifying. Pain is all of him that I have left. If my heartbreak over losing him subsides...what will remain? How can I possibly hold onto him if my pain slips through my fingers? I can't bear to lose him again. Heartbreak is all that I have left, so while I hate feeling this way, I hate the idea of not feeling this way even more. When grief is all that remains, grief is what you hold onto.

Has your grief changed over time? If so, in what way, and when? I know all grief is unique, but even a vague roadmap would be helpful. Am I destined for a life of heartbreak? I can't see the possibility of an alternative. It feels as if I will never be completely happy again. When I look at pictures of our family in the days before Liam's death, I can hear an echoing whisper in the back of my mind... "this is what happiness looks like...and no matter what happens for the rest of your life, you will never feel this happy again." Please tell me, is that whisper right?

In sadness,
Evelyn

Dear Evelyn,

I wish I could answer your question. All I can do is offer my experience, my own perspective. As you stated, all grief is unique, so I don't know what your future holds. There is a general societal belief that grief lessens with time, however, this belief is based on a very surface-level understanding of grief. From my perspective, those not experiencing grief think it only encompasses deep sadness; they do not have the viewpoint to understand how nuanced, complicated, and large grief truly is.

Before I lost Maddie, I also thought grief was limited to heartache. I had a picture in my head of crying for days, then slowly emerging from a mourning period, slightly more somber and wiser than before. I had no idea of the intensity this particular kind of heartache could bring. I had no idea grief would cause me to fall to my knees sobbing in the shower or that I could cry so hard my head would pound and the blood vessels in my eyes would burst. I had no idea my heart could literally ache and begin to skip beats. I had no idea my heart and mind could endure such intense pain. My ignorance wasn't limited to comprehending the depths of heartache, however...there was more that I didn't know. I didn't know grief isn't only defined by great sadness...that it is also composed of anger, denial, guilt, joy, and laughter. I had no idea how complicated grief is. So I will say this, my grief has not lessened with time. Rather, it has expanded to make room for the complexity of a broken, yet somehow still beating, heart.

In the beginning of my grief, I only had room for heartbreak and denial. In those early days, I didn't even have room for anger, although I know that varies greatly by person and circumstance. I was so overwhelmed with the loss of my daughter that it was all I could do to acknowledge she had died. When I did acknowledge it, I was crashed into a deeper canyon of heartache than I had ever imagined. My heart truly shattered in those days, and I developed heart palpitations from the pain.

As time passed, the shape of my grief changed. My grief over Maddie certainly didn't lessen, but it altered. One day I found I could smile. Another day I surprised myself with a laugh. Both of those instances were immediately followed by soul-crushing guilt. How could I laugh? My baby had died. How could I find joy in a world that my daughter would never see? I was inundated with deep, internal feelings of wrong-doing and shame. When I tried to explain these feelings to the non-grieving, they offered surface level platitudes— "You shouldn't feel bad about smiling, she wouldn't want you to be sad, you know." My shame over my own confusion worsened, and I immediately withdrew my heart from these conversations. I found myself in a dark, lonely world, trying to grapple with the changing shape of my grief.

Grief is a perpetual shape-shifter. However, and here's the misunderstood part, its changing shape doesn't necessarily translate into its depth lessening. When non-grievers see your grief change shape, they think that means you are emerging from the dark hole of your grief and that your loss no longer holds the same pain. They think you are "getting over" the death of your loved one. In reality, of course, you have simply expanded your emotional footprint. Your heart can, and does, encompass heart-altering pain, as well as brief moments of joy. You don't miss any less, you just learn how to miss while also holding joy.

As time passed, the moments of joy came more frequently for me, yet I still held deep guilt over experiencing them. It wasn't until I learned to find Maddie in my joy that I was able to embrace it. Maddie wasn't only loss. Maddie wasn't only pain. She was a gift. She was a gift made of love— she came from our laughter and delight, and from our immense love for each other. She may have only been here a short while, but she brought so much happiness in that time...and even now, when I think of her, it is with both heartbreak and a tender sweet joy at her memory. I will never stop missing her. I don't believe my heart will ever stop aching, or that I will ever miss her less. And yet...and yet I now can find delight in the world. Because when I touch joy, I touch Maddie. My grief has shape shifted. It hasn't lessened, it has grown. It has expanded to encompass the deep complexity of missing someone you love so much that even their absence cannot erase the elation they bring to your heart.

I believe your mother's statement about your grief changing over time was simultaneously both erroneous and accurate. You will still feel a deep sadness for years to come, likely for the rest of your life...AND you will also feel great joy. Your grief will not lessen, it will change. Grief is not only sadness. It also encompasses the joy that love brings.

So, to answer your question...I do not know what your future happiness holds. Your future will likely hold moments of great joy, and it will also hold moments of great heartache. I am constantly aware Maddie should be present in our lives and constantly miss her, whether I am experiencing moments of sadness or joy. And yet, I also am able to be deeply, truly happy. In a very real way, I am able to be both broken-hearted and joyful. My heart has evolved the ability to hold both of these emotions at once.

Maddie grew my heart. She grew it in a way that only the loss of someone you love with your entire heart can. I know you can understand this because I know Liam has grown your heart as well. We lost our children, and that is wrong, and terrible, and unfair. We also loved them, and, more importantly, love them still, and will love them forever. Love cannot only hold sadness. Its very nature requires a seed of joy. And so, we hold heartbreak and joy concurrently. These two forces are constantly pulling at us, shaping our grief in new ways on a daily basis. Some days the loss will pull stronger, some days the joy. But they will both be there, forever. We cannot ever truly lose our children because we will never stop loving them. We carry them forward with us. They will live on through our hearts, our words, and our actions.

Our babies came from love and joy. We will forever miss them AND we will forever delight in the fact of their existence. My Maddie will forever break my heart and will also forever bring me great joy. And so, when I need to find her, I will look for her in joy. She will live on in me, and in the goodness and light she brought to the world.

With tenderness,
Sarah

As the days since Kegan's birth have turned into years, I have felt a subtle shift in how I approach his death. In the early days of losing him, I lived in a state of constant denial. My mind couldn't begin to comprehend the death of a child, and beyond that, Kegan himself couldn't possibly be dead. I continually cycled through the agony of losing him anew as my heart refused to accept the reality of his death. As time has passed, I have slowly explored the reality that my son is, in fact, dead. While I may never fully accept the truth of his passing, while the shock of losing him may never fully wear off, and while there may forever be a part of me that anticipates waking to a house bursting with the laughter of two living children, I also now understand that that will never be my reality. Instead, I have integrated his loss into me, allowing him to live on through my being.

Kegan's existence has changed the world. He has changed the lives of an untold number of people in ways both explicit and subtle. Practically, Kegan has undoubtedly saved other children from death. Due to his existence, SMFM now formally acknowledges iSUA as a risk factor for stillbirth and recommends increased monitoring of iSUA pregnancies. While there is still work to be done on this front (most notably allowing delivery at 37 weeks gestation, when term pregnancy is reached), Kegan has allowed other families to bring home living babies instead of a box of keepsakes. Thanks to Kegan, other families will be allowed to raise their respective sons and daughters. For families who were not granted this privilege, for families who were cursed with the agony of losing their child to stillbirth, Kegan has a gift as well. Thanks to our sweet boy, Kegan's Law exists and, provided they live in the state of Washington, these families will be able to obtain a birth certificate for their stillborn child. And finally, for those completely separate from the world of pregnancy complications and child loss, Kegan may still make an impact through Kegan's Kindness, through the acts of goodness and charity that friends and family conduct in his memory every year. Kegan has allowed forests to be cleaned up, meals to be bought for the homeless, women and children in domestic violence shelters to be clothed, and kittens and puppies in animal shelters to be fed. He has, without a doubt, practically, demonstrably changed the world for the better.

Kegan has done more than change the world through observable acts, however. He changed *us.* He changed his sister, his father, his mother, his grandparents, his aunts, his uncles, his cousins, every friend we met or will meet, and countless strangers who have heard his story. He changed the world through the simple act of existing. He changed our world and the world of countless others. A baby's parents don't have to update medical guidelines or pass laws for their baby to change the world. Our babies change us, and they change the universe, whether they live or not. Our task is to see them in the unfolding of life and love around us.

In the beginning, I constantly yearned for a simple change in fate. I dreamt of going back in time and going into labor at 37 weeks, or even earlier. What was prematurity, after all, when compared to death? What were a few days or even weeks in the NICU when compared to the permanence of a gravestone? I found myself wishing for days in the hospital over the eternal silence of the morgue. While this yearning hasn't in any way lessened with time, I have slowly reconciled myself to the fact that I cannot change the past. I can't undo Kegan's death. I can't go into labor early, I can't spend weeks nursing my child in the NICU, I can't change the fact that he was, and always will be, born dead.

As time has passed, I have learned to stop focusing on the what-ifs of death, and to instead focus on the chances of life. I will never be able to piece my heart back together, it will forever have a Kegan-shaped hole in it. But that doesn't mean that my heart cannot love, nor that it cannot experience joy or laughter. I have learned that I can carry Kegan into that joy and laughter and see him in moments of happiness. I have a very distinct memory of turning to my husband around three years after losing our son and remarking, "We brought Kegan into this world because we were so happy. We were overwhelmed with joy and love for each other and for Keira, and we wanted more. And so, if he was made of joy, if joy is where he came from, joy is where I'll look for him." And my husband, my wonderful, patient, emotionally-reserved-engineer-of-a-husband, wordlessly absorbed his wife's sentiment with a smile and a hug.

I feel closest to Kegan when I experience joy. It took a long time to reach this point; initially I felt deep guilt, as if I were betraying my son or his memory when I experienced any sort of happiness. The guilt-laden cliches of "he wouldn't want you to be unhappy" that many would offer certainly didn't help matters, instead they only enraged and backed me further into a dark cave of grief, loneliness, and anger. Slowly, ever so slowly, however, I learned to disregard the advice or sentiments that those who had never buried a child offer and to instead focus on what felt right to our family, on what felt right to me. I learned it was ok to be angry, it was ok to be sad, it was ok to feel cheated. And I also learned it was ok to laugh, and to feel love and joy. I learned I could love my life and the people in it, while also desperately wishing that my life had played out differently. I learned I could hold space for love, gratitude, anger, and sadness, all in the same breath.

There is a misconception that we, the grieving, have to find meaning in our loved one's death, learning joy and gratitude for the lessons their death has taught us in order to "heal" and "move on" from our broken hearts. I would like to challenge this notion. We do not have to "move on" from our children and we certainly do not have to learn joy or gratitude for their deaths. I wish a million times over that I had Kegan in my arms as opposed to the lessons his death has taught me. I do not have to find a silver lining in his death. And, if I do learn how to carry lessons from his death forward with me, that certainly doesn't negate the pain of losing him. The idea that we should be grateful for the "lessons" or "strength" our children's death have brought us is an idea rooted in the deep discomfort of those who have never experienced the soul-wrenching loss of a child. I am not grateful for my son's death, I am not grateful for being forced to learn how to survive the cremation of my child, I am not grateful I have a pristine urn instead of a sticky, loud, laughing little boy. And yet…I am still grateful. I am grateful for Kegan. I am grateful for his existence, no matter how short it may have been. I am grateful for the love, joy, and empathy my son has brought into the life of everyone he has touched. Kegan's impact on the world is not rooted in his death, rather, it is rooted in his own sweet self and in our love and joy for him.

The Harvard psychologist J. William Worden outlines four tasks for the grieving. These tasks are dynamic and stand in stark comparison to the popularly recognized, more rigidly defined five stages of grief in the Kübler-Ross model (denial, anger, bargaining, depression, and acceptance). Notably, the more recognizable Kübler-Ross model was originally proposed as five stages of grief for the *dying*, not those who have been left behind, so this model is not directly applicable to the bereaved. Worden's tasks of mourning, in contrast, help the griever integrate their loss into their lives, allowing them to carry the memory of their loved one with them into their future. Worden proposes that these tasks are necessary to "re-establish equilibrium" and find future joy and fulfillment within our lives. He emphasizes these tasks aren't stages of grief, but rather are the work of grief, and can be revisited multiple times over a person's lifetime. While I personally find these tasks to be a little academic and sterile for the messy work of grieving your most loved people, I appreciate the goals at the root of them. Worden is encouraging us to take ownership of our grief, to not passively accept a lifetime of heartbreak, but to work to integrate our missing loved ones into our presents and our futures. As someone who refuses to leave her son in the past, but also desperately longs for sunny days with her daughter, this idea resonates. And so, Worden's four tasks of grief are:

    1) Accept the reality of the loss
    2) Walk through the pain of grief
    3) Adjust to an environment where our loved one is missing
    4) Develop an enduring connection with our loved one to be able to move forward with our life

What does each of these tasks mean? How do we practically work to achieve them and what if we find certain tasks harder or more challenging to address? How will these tasks impact our futures? What do they mean for our grief, and what do they mean for our joys?

Task One: Accept the reality of the loss. This first task requires us to acknowledge and come to terms with the fact that our children are, and will remain, dead. Like many grieving parents, I was in denial after Kegan's death. I could not accept the reality that he was dead and kept waiting to wake up from the nightmare that I was trapped in. By not integrating the reality of my son's death, I was constantly forcing myself to relive his dying, which made my life even more painful and heartbreaking. I was unable to accept the truth of Kegan's death for a myriad of reasons, but one of the most notable was the unstated fear that accepting his death implied a tacit approval of it. It turns out, however, that we don't have to approve or agree with something to accept it, we just have to acknowledge the reality with which we are confronted.

Task Two: Walk through the pain of grief. We cannot avoid the pain of grief. There is no way around, over, or under grief, there is only a path through it. If we avoid our pain, either by numbing it with alcohol, burying ourselves in work, or simply pushing it down and not addressing it, it will find alternative, more harmful, ways to manifest in our lives. We can't avoid the pain of grief, grief demands to be seen, it demands to be felt. The only way to progress through grief is to grieve.

Task Three: Adjust to an environment where our loved one is missing. After the initial mourning period has passed, we will have to return to our everyday lives. Bills still have to be paid, groceries still have to be bought, children still have school and extracurriculars, and romantic relationships still need to be nourished. It is normal to feel as if the mundane activities of life are unimportant after the soul-wrenching loss of a child, and yet...everyday life will still exist. And so, we will need to adjust to performing the tasks of living while carrying our grief with us. This extraordinary act of simply functioning in everyday life while drowning in heartbreak may require us to ask for help or to learn new skills. I have found a therapist to be extremely helpful in learning how to navigate everyday tasks while simultaneously carrying my immense grief for my son.

Task Four: Develop an enduring connection with our loved one to be able to move forward with our life. I personally would prefer this task to focus less on "moving forward" and more on "finding joy in the life we are living." My goal is not to leave my son behind me, it is to bring him forward *with me* into a life filled with laughter, love, joy, and yes, grief. This task describes the need to develop an enduring connection with your lost loved one—this can mean varying things to different people, but to me, this speaks of holding your child in your heart through memories, thoughts, and rituals. I find immense healing in the power of rituals, in the constant inclusion of Kegan in our lives and our family through simple traditions, whether that tradition is participating in Kegan's Kindness on his birthday, or simply placing his stocking on the mantle at Christmas. We keep Kegan continually present in our hearts, which allows us to experience joy and love without the fear of leaving him behind. While it may feel as if our lives ended when Kegan died, (and in truth, the versions of ourselves and our lives that existed before he died *did* end), we are in fact still living, and our daughter is living as well. We have a great deal of joy to still experience in the world, and we can bring his memory forward with us into that joy. My hope for Keira, Karol, and myself is that we can still experience the immense joy life has to offer, *and that it is in those moments of joy that we will feel most connected to Kegan*. After all, as I told Karol, it is from love and joy that Kegan originally came, and it is in love and joy that we can feel him again.

Grief is unique to the griever. While academic formulas of mourning or checklists of grieving may exist, in reality, there is not a universal right or best way to grieve. Similarly, there is not a prize of "closure" to be reached, or an end of grief to strive for. There is simply love, love flowing out of you with nowhere to go and no one to accept it. So, what do you do with all that love? What do you do with the love you want to give your baby and cannot? For us, we have chosen to give it away. We give it to our loved ones, to strangers, and yes, to ourselves. It turns out, love is really all that grief is, and that love is yours to do with whatever you want.

Grief is a condition of your entire being. It is a condition of the heart, of the mind, and of the body. It fills your soul with emptiness, disrupts your thoughts, and causes your body to ache. We cannot think ourselves out of grief, nor can we take a pill to cure it. We have to feel it. We have to grieve our way through grief. It is the only path forward. We have to look the massive hole in our lives and hearts head on and rebuild ourselves around it. This is hard. It takes time, it takes tears, and, sadly, it is a never-ending work. I will grieve forever. My grief today doesn't look the way it did four years ago, but it is not any smaller, it is not any less. It may not be as raw as it used to be, but my sadness over losing my son has not in any way diminished. I will grieve Kegan until my dying day. The shape of that grief may change, but it will always be there.

In the beginning, my grief only had space for pain. It only had space for heartbreak, tears, and disbelief. As time has passed, my grief has altered. It still holds heartbreak, it still holds tears, and, yes, it still holds a level of disbelief, but that is not all. Now it also holds joy, and laughter, and memories of goodness and love done in my son's name. As we have reshaped our lives in memory of our son, he has reshaped our hearts and our grief in his image. I now know that while I will always deeply miss my son, I will also have days where I experience joy. This does not mean I have left Kegan behind, or that I am over his death. Rather, it simply means that my heart, mind, and body have found a way to carry him forward with me.

Kegan will live on as long as I live in his name. I cannot truly ever lose him because he has changed me. He has changed my heart and my mind, he has changed the way I see the world, and the way I love. The world is a better place for my son's existence. While he may never experience the world, the world has experienced him. We will live on in his memory. We will be his legacy. We will love in his name.

I consider my son to be a miracle. You see, once upon a time, my son died. He died, and then he was born. And then, he spread love and light beyond my wildest imaginings. And so, once upon a time, my son changed the world.

All of our children change the world, whether they live or not. They change us. Their final legacy to us is love. And love never, ever dies.

Journal Prompt:

How has your grief changed over time? What shape would you like your grief to take in the future? Are there any steps you can take to bring this shape into reality? What messages would you share with your future self in five or ten years, and what messages do you think your future self would impart to you now?

KEGAN'S KINDNESS

Our family would like to invite you to participate in Kegan's Kindness on or around the anniversary of Kegan's death (November 6) or birth (November 7). On these days, our friends and family join us in performing acts of intentional kindness and charity in Kegan's memory. Kegan's Kindness acts can be any act of goodness, from volunteering at shelters, to donating needed goods, to performing trail cleanups, to simply buying a stranger coffee or a meal. We have been amazed to hear stories of Kegan's Kindness from across the globe and are so honored and grateful for the many acts, both large and small, done in our boy's memory. We know Kegan would have changed the world for the better; through your goodness and kindness, he still can.

Thank you again, from the bottom of our hearts, and much love to you all.

With love,
Terrell, Karol, and Keira

I think it's beautiful how a star's light
travels the universe, long after it dies.
That's what I want to be in this world—
Someone whose light lingers on after I'm gone.

~John Mark Green

STILLBIRTH AND GRIEF RESOURCES

Stillbirth and Grief Resources

Organization	URL	Focus
Star Legacy Foundation (U.S.A.)	https://starlegacyfoundation.org/	U.S. based stillbirth research and advocacy; an organization dedicated to uncovering the causes of stillbirth to prevent future stillbirths and to advocating for bereaved families
Now I Lay Me Down to Sleep	https://www.nowilaymedowntosleep.org/	Bereavement portraiture; an organization that provides the gift of remembrance photography to parents experiencing the death of a baby
Seleni	https://www.seleni.org/	Maternal mental health and family building challenges; an institute dedicated to providing psychotherapy to families experiencing mental health challenges related to building their families, stillbirth, and infant loss
Compassionate Friends	https://www.compassionatefriends.org/	Family support; a support group dedicated to supporting parents, siblings, and grandparents after the death of a child
Share	https://nationalshare.org/	Pregnancy and infant loss support; a community for anyone who has experienced the loss of a baby; Share serves parents, siblings, grandparents, friends, and healthcare providers
National Alliance for Children's Grief	https://childrengrieve.org/	Child grief support; an organization that serves children experiencing grief
Centering	https://centering.org/	Books/resources on grief; a collection of books/resources dedicated to the topic of grief
Tommy's (U.K.)	https://www.tommys.org/baby-loss-support/stillbirth-information-and-support	U.K. based support and advocacy; an organization based in the U.K. dedicated to supporting and advocating for families after stillbirth
SANDS (Australia)	https://www.sands.org.au/	Australia based pregnancy and infant loss support; an organization in Australia dedicated to supporting and advocating for bereaved families

BeliEve Foundation	https://thebelievefoundation.org/	Financial support after baby loss; an organization dedicated to supporting families and advocacy groups through financial challenges associated with stillbirth
International Stillbirth Alliance	https://www.stillbirthalliance.org/	International stillbirth advocacy; an organization supporting international advocacy for bereaved families and research into the causes of stillbirth
GriefShare	https://www.griefshare.org/	Online support groups; international online grief support groups offering weekly meetings
TEARS Foundation	https://thetearsfoundation.org/	Financial support after baby loss; an organization dedicated to supporting families and advocacy groups through financial challenges associated with child loss
PUSH for Empowered Pregnancy (U.S.A.)	https://www.pushpregnancy.org/	U.S. based stillbirth advocacy; an organization seeking to decrease stillbirth in the U.S.A. through interfacing with researchers, physicians, and legislators

REFERENCES:

Journal Articles:

American College of Obstetricians and Gynecologists. "Avoidance of Nonmedically Indicated Early-Term Deliveries and Associated Neonatal Morbidities." *Obstet Gyneco,* vol. 133, no. 2, 2019, pp. E156–e163.

American College of Obstetricians and Gynecologists and Society for Maternal Fetal Medicine. "Management of Stillbirth: Obstetric Care Consensus No, 10." *Obstet Gynecol*. Vol 135, no. 3, 2020, pp. e110–e132.

Avelin P, Erlandsson K, Hildingsson I, Bremborg AD, Rådestad I. Make the Stillborn Baby and the Loss Real for the Siblings: Parents' Advice on How the Siblings of a Stillborn Baby Can Be Supported. *J Perinat Educ,* vol 21, 2012, pp 90–98. doi:10.1891/1058-1243.21.2.90.

Bramlett MD, Mosher WD. Cohabitation, Marriage, Divorce, and Remarriage in the United States. *Vital Health Stat 23,* vol 22, 2002, pp 1–93. PMID: 12183886.

Cacciatore J. Effects of Support Groups on Post Traumatic Stress Responses in Women Experiencing Stillbirth. *Omega (Westport),* vol 55, 2007, pp 71–90.

Cacciatore J, DeFrain J, Jones KLC, Jones H. Stillbirth and the Couple: A Gender-Based Exploration. *J. Fam. Soc. Work,* vol 11, 2008, 351–370.

Cacciatore J, Schnebly S, Froen JF. The effects of social support on maternal anxiety and depression after stillbirth. *Health Soc Care*

Community, vol 17, 2009, pp 167–176. doi: 10.1111/j.1365-2524.2008.00814.x.

DeBackere KJ, Hill PD, Kavanaugh KL. The parental experience of pregnancy after perinatal loss. *J Obstet Gynecol Neonatal Nurs*, vol 37, 2008, pp 525–537. doi:10.1111/j.1552-6909.2008.00275.x.

Doka KJ. Disenfranchised Grief. *Bereavement Care,* vol 18, 1999, pp 37–39.

Fernández-Sola C, Camacho-Ávila M, Hernández-Padilla JM, et al. Impact of Perinatal Death on the Social and Family Context of the Parents. *Int J Environ Res Public Health*, vol 17, 2020. doi:10.3390/ijerph17103421.

Flach, K, Gressler, NG, Marcolino, MAZ et al. "Complicated Grief After the Loss of a Baby: A Systematic Review About Risk and Protective Factors for Bereaved Women." *Trends in Psychol.,* 2022. https://doi.org/10.1007/s43076-021-00112-z.

Frøen J, et al. "Stillbirths: An Executive Summary for the Lancet's Series." *The Lancet,* vol 377, 2011. https://els-jbs-prod-cdn.jbs.elsevierhealth.com/pb/assets/raw/Lancet/stories/series/stillbirths/stillbirths.pdf.

Frøen J, et al. Ending preventable stillbirths: An Executive Summary for The Lancet's Series. *The Lancet*, vol 387, 2016, pp 703–716. https://www.thelancet.com/series/ending-preventable-stillbirths.

Glass R. "Is Grief a Disease? Sometimes." *JAMA,* vol. 293, no. 21, 2005, pp. 2658–2660. doi:10.1001/jama.293.21.2658.

Gold KJ, Sen A, Hayward RA. Marriage and Cohabitation Outcomes after Pregnancy Loss. *Pediatrics*, vol 125, 2010, pp e1202-e1207. doi: 10.1542/peds.2009-3081.

Hammad IA, Blue NR, Allshouse AA, et al. Umbilical Cord Abnormalities and Stillbirth. *Obstet Gynecol*, vol 135, 2020, pp 644–652. doi:10.1097/AOG.0000000000003676.

Heazell A, et al. "Stillbirth is Associated with Perceived Alterations in Fetal Activity – Findings from an International Case Control Study." *BMC Pregnancy Childbirth,* vol 17, no 1, 2017, pp. 369.

Heller SS, Zeanah CH. Attachment Disturbance in Infants Born Subsequent to Perinatal Loss: A Pilot Study. *Infant Ment Health J,* vol 20, 1999.

Horesh, D, et al. "To Lose an Unborn Child: Post-Traumatic Stress Disorder and Major Depressive Disorder Following Pregnancy Loss among Israeli Women." *General Hospital Psychiatry,* vol. 53, 2018, pp. 95–100, https://doi.org/10.1016/j.genhosppsych.2018.02.003.

Hughes P, Turton P, Hopper E et al. Disorganised Attachment Behaviour Among Infants Born Subsequent to Stillbirth. *J Child Psychol Psychitat,* vol 42, 2001.

Hutti MH. Social and Professional Support Needs of Families after Perinatal Loss. *J Obstet Gynecol Neonatal Nurs*, vol 34, 2005, pp 630–638.

Kersting A, Wagner B. "Complicated Grief after Perinatal Loss." *Dialogues Clin Neurosci*, vol. 14, no. 2, 2012, pp. 187–194.

Koopmans L, Wilson T, Cacciatore J, Flenady V. Support for Mothers, Fathers and Families after Perinatal Death. *Cochrane Database Syst Rev,* 2013. doi: 10.1002/14651858.CD000452.pub3.

Lasker, J. N., & Toedter, L. J. Predicting Outcomes after Pregnancy Loss: Results from Studies Using the Perinatal Grief Scale. *Illness, Crisis & Loss,* vol *8,* 2000, pp 350–372. https://doi.org/10.1177/105413730000800402

McCreight BS. A grief ignored: Narratives of Pregnancy Loss from a Male Perspective. *Soc Health Illness,* vol 26, 2004.

Murray JA, Terry DJ. Parental Reactions to Infant Death: The Effects of Resources and Coping. *J Soc Clin Psychol,* vol 18, 1999, 341–369.

Nicholson JM. The 39-Week Rule and Term Stillbirth: Beneficence, Autonomy, and the Ethics of the Current Restrictions on Early-Term Labor Induction in the US. *BMC Pregnancy Childbirth,* vol 15, 2015. doi:10.1186/1471-2393-15-S1-A9.

Nicholson J, et al. "US Term Stillbirth Rates and the 39-Week Rule: A Cause for Concern?" *Am J Obstet Gynecol,* vol. 214, iss. 5, 2016, pp. e1–9. doi: 10.1016/j.ajog.2016.02.019.

O'Leary J, Thorwick C. Fathers' Perspectives during Pregnancy, Postperinatal Loss. *J Obstet Gynecol Neonat Nurs,* vol 35, 2006.

Obst KL, Oxlad M, Due C, Middleton P. Factors Contributing to Men's Grief Following Pregnancy Loss and Neonatal Death: Further

Development of an Emerging Model in an Australian Sample. *BMC Pregnancy Childbirth*, vol 21, 2021. doi:10.1186/s12884-020-03514-6.

Pilliod R, et al. "Association of Widespread Adoption of the 39-Week Rule with Overall Mortality Due to Stillbirth and Infant Death." *JAMA Pediatr,* vol. 173, no.12, 2019, pp. 1180–1185.

Pollock D, et al. "Understanding Stillbirth Stigma: A Scoping Literature Review." *Women Birth*, vol. 33, no. 3, 2022, pp. 207–218.

Samuelsson M, Radestad I, Segesten K: A Waste of Life: Fathers' Experience of Losing a Child Before Birth. *Birth,* vol 28, 2001.

Sherer DM, Al-Haddad S, Cheng R, Dalloul M. Current Perspectives of Prenatal Sonography of Umbilical Cord Morphology. *Int J Womens Health*, vol 13, 2021, pp 939–971. doi:10.2147/IJWH.S278747.

Umphrey LR, Cacciatore J. Coping with the Ultimate Deprivation: Narrative Themes in a Parental Bereavement Support Group. *Omega (Westport),* vol 63, 2011, pp 141–160.

Wagner S, et al. "Labor Induction at 39 Weeks Compared with Expectant Management in Low-Risk Parous Women." *Am J Perinatol,* vol 29, no. 5, 2020, pp. 519–525, doi: 10.1055/s-0040-1716711.

Walling A. "Elective Induction Doubles Cesarean Delivery Rate." *Am Fam Physician,* vol. 61, no, 4, 2000, pp. 1173.

Williams C, Munson D, Zupancic J, Kirpalani H. Supporting Bereaved Parents: Practical Steps in Providing Compassionate Perinatal and Neonatal End-of-Life Care: A North American Perspective. *Semin Fetal Neonatal Med,* vol 13, 2008, pp 335–340.

Wilson DM, Underwood L, Errasti-Ibarrondo B. A Scoping Research Literature Review to Map the Evidence on Grief Triggers. *Soc Sci Med, vol 282,* 2021. doi: 10.1016/j.socscimed.2021.114109.

Worth N. Becoming a Father to a Stillborn Child. *Clin Nurs Res,* vol 6, 1997.

Zeanah CH, Danis B, Hirshberg L, et al. Initial Adaptation in Mothers and Fathers Following Perinatal Loss. *Infant Mental Health J,* vol 16, 1995.

Books:

Worden, JW. Grief Counseling and Grief Therapy: A Handbook for the Mental Health Practitioner, Fourth Edition, New York City, Springer, 2009.

Websites:

American Psychiatric Association. "What is Posttraumatic Stress Disorder?" Nov 2022, https://www.psychiatry.org/patients-families/ptsd/what-is-ptsd#:~:text=People%20with%20PTSD%20have%20intense,or%20estranged%20from%20other%20people.

Doka, K. 3 C's for Holiday Grief. December 2020. https://www.taps.org/articles/2020/holiday-grief/?gclid=Cj0KCQjw1vSZBhDuARIsAKZlijSPK6g5ZcX-yksRJmUa-BqK_dg-pumfHTXQ8P-puBXBS-GATzzHjZoaAvn6EALw_wc.

Gleeson L. "How Grief Manifests in the Body." Shapes of Grief, 2017. https://shapesofgrief.com/blog/how-grief-manifests-in-the-body-by-liz-gleeson/.

Gold K. "The Complex Costs of Stillbirth." Institute of Healthcare Policy and Innovation, University of Michigan, 2016. https://ihpi.umich.edu/news/complex-costs-stillbirth.

Hughes V. "Shades of Grief: When Does Mourning Become a Mental Illness?" Scientific American, 2011. https://www.scientificamerican.com/article/shades-of-grief/.

Leon I. "Helping Families Cope with Perinatal Loss." Glob Lib Women's Med. 2008. Available at: www.glowm.com/index.html?p=glowm.cml/section_view&articleid=417#15251.

Muller R. "Grieving the Loss of a Child: The Five Stage Myth." Psychology Today, Sussex Publishers, 2015. https://www.psychologytoday.com/us/blog/talking-about-trauma/201506/grieving-the-loss-child-the-five-stage-myth.

National Institutes of Health. "Post-traumatic Stress Disorder." National Institute of Mental Health, May 2022, https://www.nimh.nih.gov/health/topics/post-traumatic-stress-disorder-ptsd#:~:text=thoughts%20of%20revenge.-,Risk%20Factors,disaster%2C%20or%20other%20serious%20event.

Now I Lay Me Down to Sleep. "Now I Lay Me Down to Sleep." Accessed March 2022. https://www.nowilaymedowntosleep.org/.

Siegel A. "Stillbirth as a Trauma." Psychology Today, Sussex Publishers, Nov 2019, https://www.psychologytoday.com/us/blog/traumatized/201911/stillbirth-trauma.

Star Legacy Foundation. "Star Legacy Foundation. Accessed March 2022. https://starlegacyfoundation.org/.

Star Legacy Foundation. "US 2017 Stillbirth Scorecard." Accessed March 2022. https://starlegacyfoundation.org/us-2017-stillbirth-scorecard/.

The BeliEve Foundation. "About Us." Accessed March 2022. https://thebelievefoundation.org/about-us/.

The Center for Prolonged Grief. "Prolonged Grief: Diagnosis." Columbia University, 2017. https://complicatedgrief.columbia.edu/professionals/complicated-grief-professionals/diagnosis/.

The Tears Foundation. "Who We Are." Accessed March 2022. https://thetearsfoundation.org/.

Tommy's. "Having a Post-mortem after a Stillbirth." Accessed March 2022. https://www.tommys.org/baby-loss-support/stillbirth-information-and-support/having-post-mortem-after-stillbirth.

Vitas Healthcare. Coping with Grief During the Holidays. Accessed October 2022. https://www.vitas.com/family-and-caregiver-support/grief-and-bereavement/holidays-and-grief/coping-with-grief-during-the-holidays.

Washington State Department of Health. "Ordering a Stillbirth Record." October 2022. https://doh.wa.gov/licenses-permits-and-certificates/vital-records/ordering-vital-record/stillbirth-record.

Washington State Hospital Association. "Elective Delivery 37 to less than 39 Weeks Gestational Age." Accessed April 2022. https://www.wsha.org/quality-safety/projects/safe-deliveries/elective-delivery-37-to-less-than-39-weeks-gestational-age/.

ABOUT THE AUTHOR

Terrell Hatzilias, PhD is a bereaved mother, stillbirth advocate, medical writer, and neuroscientist. She is the proud mother of a strong, smart, kind little girl, as well as the grieving mother of a stillborn baby boy.

Dr. Hatzilias is originally from Northern Virginia, where her lifelong love of science and research began as a student at the Thomas Jefferson High School for Science and Technology. She earned her bachelor's degree from Duke University, where she majored in Biology and minored in Psychology, thus beginning an obsession with anything even tangentially related to biopsychology or neuroscience. Dr. Hatzilias earned her doctorate in Neuroscience from Emory University, focusing on neurodegenerative diseases and protein folding. It was during a subsequent post-doctoral position at the Georgia Institute of Technology that Dr. Hatzilias discovered medical writing, and subsequently left academia to become a writer.

The Hatzilias family was living near Seattle, WA when Kegan Christopher Hatzilias was stillborn at term in 2018. Following Kegan's death, Dr. Hatzilias began a campaign to prevent other babies from suffering the same fate, which resulted in the Society for Maternal-Fetal Medicine updating its guidelines on managing isolated single umbilical artery pregnancies. She also successfully led a group of bereaved mothers in the state of Washington in lobbying the legislature to pass a law allowing issuance of a Certificate of Birth Resulting in Stillbirth.

When she is not writing or advocating for stillbirth prevention, Terrell enjoys volunteering at her daughter's school, drinking hot tea, and attempting to train the family dog. She loves to travel and can't resist a good cozy mystery to keep her company on the plane. Terrell will forever be grateful for her supportive husband, loving daughter, and of course, for the memory of her beautiful son.

Keep in touch with Dr. Hatz via the web at:
Instagram: still_his_mama
LinkedIn: https://www.linkedin.com/in/terrell-hatzilias-18b07a30/

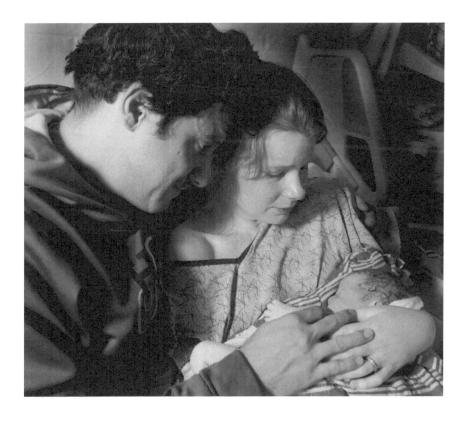